VERNACULAR HISTORY SERIES

The 'Vernacular History' series of books and booklets, of which this is number six, reflects a picture of life 'as it really was'–or at least as it seemed to be to those living it at the time: and the time may be in past centuries up to the quite recent past. There is no precise time of 'cut-off' and the intention of the series is to show life as it was experienced by those involved–and perhaps to correct impressions given by fictional events in a fictional landscape. The series is similar to the **Life in Lincolnshire** series of titles except that the scene is not necessarily based on a Lincolnshire setting and titles may vary very considerably in length. The criterion for acceptance into the series is essentially personal experience. A polished literary style may or may not be present–veracity is mandatory.

These accounts may sometimes be the work of men and women experienced in writing but also they may sometimes be the work of those who have not had the benefits of formal education and have never previously written for publication. So far as practicable editing has been kept to a minimum with the account being presented in the words of the author and any illustration being from contemporary material. Although memories are not infallible, and some recollected detail may have become embroidered with the passage of time, the books are intended as factual records of the experiences of men and women, in all social groups, which might not otherwise have been preserved.

THE ERRAND BOY WHO WENT TO SEA

by

VERDUN WILLOUGHBY

(KNOWN AS 'VIC')

19 99

RICHARD KAY
80 SLEAFORD ROAD • BOSTON • LINCOLNSHIRE PE21 8EU

© Verdun Willoughby 1999
First published by Richard Kay Publications 1999
ISBN 1 902882 40 7

Typeset by the publisher initially in Microsoft Word™ and PageMaker™ on an AppleMacintosh™ and output in camera-ready copy which was then manipulated via a Media Server in Bookman typeface for the body of the text. Then manipulated electronically and printed using digital technology by:

Foxe Laser
Enterprise Road • Mablethorpe • Lincolnshire. LN12 1NB

CONTENTS

ILLUSTRATIONS

ACKNOWLEDGEMENTS

We are most grateful for the pen and ink drawing 'The boy on the docks' by Mrs Jenny Reynish: to Olivia da Silva for the photograph on the front cover and to Mr Bill Collins for the photograph of the 'great freeze' 1947 (made available through the kind assistance of Mr Peter Chapman). Other photographs made available by the author or the publisher.

Some of the Steam Trawlers on which 'Vic' sailed.
'B' denotes 'before the war'. The year is only approximate.

Vessel	Owner	Fishing Destination	
S. T. *Abronia*	T.C. & F. Moss'	North Sea	'B'
" " *Aquarius*	Bacons' ?	" "	'B'
" " *Balmoral*	Queens'	" "	'B' '33
" " *Carlton*	T.C. & F. Moss'	" "	'B'
" " *Cancer*	Bacons' ?	" "	'B'
" " *Castor*	Bacons' ?	" "	'B'
" " *Clacton*	T.C. & F. Moss'	" "	'B'
" " *Curtana*	Butts'	Faroes	'B'
" " *Diamond*	T.C. & F. Moss'	North Sea	'B'
" " *Donalda*	Bacons'	Faroes	'B'
" " *Edwardian*	Butts'	White Sea	'B'
" " *Emerald*	T.C. & F. Moss'	North Sea	'B'
" " *Glen Kidston*	Croft Baker	White Sea	
" " *Gurth*	T.C. & F. Moss'	North Sea	
" " *Lacennia*	–	White Sea	
" " *Okino*	Taylors'	Faroes	
" " *Olympia*	Butts'	Faroes	
" " *Ottilie*	Derwent	North Sea	
" " *Pearl*	T.C. & F. Moss'	North Sea	'B'
" " *Prince Leo*	T.C. & F. Moss'	North Sea	
" " *Prince Victor*	T.C. & F. Moss'	North Sea	
" " *Riano*	Sleights'	North Sea	'B' '26
" " *River Witham*	Consols'	North Sea	'B'
" " *River Spey*	Bostons'	North Sea	
" " *Rononia*	Bacons'	North Sea	'B' '27
" " *Rose of England*	–	North Sea	
" " *Salacon*	Butts'	Faroes	
" " *Scooper*	Bacons'	North Sea	
" " *Staunton*	–	Faroes	'B'
" " *Strephon*	Taylors'	North Sea	
" " *Vascama*	–	White Sea	
" " *Visenda*	–	Iceland	
" " *Vizalma*	–	Iceland	
" " *War Duke*	–	North Sea	

Also several of Sleights' inshore trawlers and several seine-netters.
Records are not always available and memory can be fallible.

Errand-boy 1930

Mate *Rose of England* in the 1950s

Replica model *Rose of England* by Mr George Brown of
Weelsby Street, Grimsby, whose late father was Chief
Engineer of the ship.

At sea–fishing in the North Sea in *M/V Four Seas*

Diamond wedding on the 27th March 1997 with Her Majesty's telegram.

Grimsby Fishdocks 1947. Frozen in the dock in one of the severest winters on record.

CHAPTER 1

GRIMSBY—THE RIVERSIDE

I was born in 1916 less than a mile from the River Humber. The first house that I remember living in was in Bedford Street, Grimsby. It was about five minutes walk to Clee station, where the sands stopped the water from coming into the streets. When I was just able to walk I was taken, by my mother, to play on these sands.

After a few years I went to school in Hilda Street; then to Weelsby Street school. My school pals and neighbours, Charles Marlow, whose father was No. 1 Tug skipper on the docks; Joe Marlow; Johnny Butler; and Billy Sayers: all lived in Bedford Street and we all spent our time playing on Clee sands, as we called them.

We used to make a fishing line with one hook and throw it out into the water at high tide, catching many flat fish and eels. We were very small boys, so when we threw the line, with a piece of old iron for a lead, it only went out a few yards.

I remember the Louth flood. Bedford Street was flooded, too. Our fire in the grate went out, and my mother threw the old floor mat into the back yard. Charles and I rowed up and down the street in a wash tub, a wooden one, and Doris, a little girl friend of ours, would push us up and down the street, the water being about one foot deep.

When we were a bit older, Charles and I used to explore the sea shore. Pieces of coal we picked up we would bag and take home to help with our fires. It helped my mother, who also put potato peelings to burn with the coke that I brought from the Gas House, at a shilling a bag

Charles and I would walk to the railway bridge on Fuller Street, Cleethorpes. When the tide went out a wooden wreck showed out of the sands about two hundred yards above the low water mark–the tide went out a very long way. Looking into the receding tide very closely, we would see small Dover soles, trying to keep up with the ebbing water. We often caught small plaice, dabs, bullyheads and shrimps, in the pools of water, with our bare hands, then we'd let them swim away again. When the wreck was uncovered and the water had gone down, we could put our hands in the wooden holes in the wreck's sides, and pull the large, red crabs out. Sometimes, other lads from different parts of Grimsby would chase us away.

Between the ages of eight and ten years, Charles and I would roam about the sands, from the docks to the boating lake at Cleethorpes. In our young days, it seemed the summers were hotter and the winters colder than they are now. During the summer time, the streets were tarred frequently. A horse drawn cart with a tar sprinkler would come along spraying very hot tar all over the road, which was then covered with small stones. When the tar ran into the gutters it cooled down in strips. Charles and I would roll these up into balls, allow them to set hard, and then use them to play marbles

During the freezing winter months, we used to make slides on the road. We would take off our coats and, using them like a broom, would polish the road until it was like a piece of glass, for a stretch of maybe about twenty or thirty yards. Other kids in the street helped us when they knew that they would be allowed to slide on it as well. Sometimes, queueing up for a turn, there might be almost fifty boys and girls waiting for a turn or sliding on the street. We saw many streets with these slides, some with children still sliding well into the night.

Anyway, Charles and I would walk for hours at a time on the sands–exploring, we called it. We could collect buckets of lovely large cockles if we wished; but a horse and cart used to come down our street once a week to sell them, anyway.

'Cockles, cockles, all alive', the man would shout in our alley. 'One shilling for a small bucket full.' My mother would put salt in the bucket of cockles, then boil them afterwards. Someone came round with herrings as well; two for a penny:

2.

they came from the herring luggers landing fresh herrings in their hundreds in the Royal Dock Basin every day. The herrings were landed while stores were being taken on board. Then the drifters were away again, their nets out for the night, to return again next morning.

Charles and I trudged on until we came to the old, rusty, 'World War One' tank, not far from the old bathing pool. We used to play at soldiers with other kids, on and inside the tank, until some used it as a toilet. Then we moved further up the river where we came across a small island where the boating lake now stands. The water was not very deep so we paddled in it, finding the tide sometimes reached this island and left small flounder, plaice, bullyhead and shrimps in the water. We were always hungry, so if someone had eaten an orange and threw the peel away, we divided it between us, and that became our meal for the day—until we arrived home at night fall, then maybe some chips and peas awaited us.

Charles and I would walk from Clee Station to the Kingsway. It was a good, quiet playground for us. Along the sands, sometimes we would bump into 'Two Stick Charlie', a well known character of many years ago. He would chase the bigger lads, who liked to tease him, with the two sticks he always carried. If one of the sticks reached any of the boys he would remember it for some time—'Two Stick Charlie' threw his sticks accurately, and they hurt.

Charles and I would move off quickly to play with the crabs which lived under the Kingsway Pier, amongst the stones. The steep stone steps from the promenade seemed never to end, going down until we reached the sands. There the stones were always covered by green weed. We used to squeeze the bubbly weed and make it crack, to amuse ourselves. The bigger the crack it made the more it pleased us. We upturned the small stones and little crabs would run away and hide themselves. Clawing at the sand, they were soon out of sight. The flatties, bullies and shrimps all did their best to hide from us.

On our weekends off from school, we used to walk to Tetney

Marshes for the samphire that grows on the sand, which the wild geese and ducks live on during the winter months. We would bunch the roots together and, hanging the bunches from a small stick over our shoulders, carry the samphire all the way along the foreshore to Clee station from where we walked over the allotments to our home, where my mother boiled the samphire for us.

On the way we'd often pass crews from the shanikars (small fishing boats) digging for sandworms, which they used as bait for their line-fishing. Each vessel's crew would dig in a circle, pile the sand in the middle and put their worms in a large wooden bucket.

Their vessels were left high and dry on the sands as the tide went down, so that the crews could red lead the bottoms of their boats, which I believe Tommy Cotler, Mr Farrow and several boat owners did each year, to preserve their boats. Tommy, Billy, George, Harry, Charles, Joey, Squire and many more who explored and played on our sea shore are not with us any more. Some were lost during the war, mine-sweeping, or lost at sea, fishing. Charles and Harry went to live in Australia, where their sons now do the fishing.

It seems very quiet now that 10,000 fishermen have gone.

MY INTRODUCTION TO FISHING

It was the year 1929 when Arthur Tideswell, a local butcher, sent me to the Royal Dock Office for a permit to fish with rod and line off the West Pier, an old wooden jetty to which the drifters tied up during the herring season.

Calling at the Royal Dock Basin were cargo boats coming through the basin to enter the Royal Dock, the *S.S.Bury*, S.S.*Accrington*, S.S.*Marylebone*, the 'butter boats', 'water boat', G.C.R.A. and many more big trading ships coming and going to the continent and back each week; weekly boats we used to call them. Then there was the *Sir Herbert Miles*, a lovely clean ship that any sailor would have been proud to have sailed in, its mooring ropes all tidily coiled on the deck, which was scrubbed every morning, and its wooden rails sand-scrubbed like the deck, white as snow–beautiful. I often wonder where she finished up during the war.

The price of the fishing permit was one shilling. The butcher said he would take me fishing but we had to dig for lugworms from the Clee sands first. There were men in groups of five or six digging for their own boats which were ready for sea. I had a look inside one of the boats and saw a pile of sand in the hold. One of the crewmen uptipped a full bucket of lugworms on this pile of sand, saying that it would keep them alive whilst at sea.

Fishing from the pier, we caught many eels and flounders; during winter we caught some nice codling. Sometimes the bait froze so hard that we had a job to bait up. Large lumps of ice floating on the river hindered us in fishing, taking the line as it floated by.

A diver, going down to inspect the lock gates because they had been difficult to close, came up to tell the Dock Master that so many eels had accumulated that they prevented the gates from closing. I watched as he came up.

Small fishing vessels would trawl outside the docks, going as far as Immingham or beyond to catch small sprats. When they came in the lock pits we saw that their fish rooms were full and the decks full of sprats, just for a couple of hours work. We asked for some to use as bait, but we did not catch anything with them.

I saw Mr. Swan, the jeweller, and his American friend, fishing with mussel for bait. The Yank hadn't seen a lugworm before, so I gave them some to fish with.

As time went on, more people started to fish from the pier. Fishing clubs were formed; my record catch of 42 eels was caught by one hook and line during one period. It was recorded in the *Angling Times*; all were caught at Charlton's

Creek–which was on the west side of the Royal Dock.

I have met anglers from all over the country who came to fish the West Pier and I have seen the fins of sharks swimming around us there.

The fish which I have myself seen caught in the river by line or net include:

River smelts–a small variety.

Sea smelts–a larger fish. Both smell like cucumbers.

Herring, odd ones.

Mullet, in hundreds

Cod, in hundreds.

Plaice, in hundreds.

Dabs, odd ones.

Eels, in hundreds.

Salmon, just the odd one washed ashore.

Bass, quite a lot seen swimming.

Soles, in hundreds.

Skate, a few.

Flounders, in hundreds.

Pollock, a few on hard ground.

Eel pouts–not edible.

Whiting, a lot of small ones.

Haddock–I have never seen one caught here.

Conger eel–one washed up; frozen it weighed 32lb.

THE HUMBER FOGS

When we were at school, now many years ago, less than a quarter of a mile from the tide's edge, one would hear a remark by one of the boys, 'Is your father working yet?' The answer to that might be. 'Yes, a regular one now, sweeping the fog off the Humber.'

As a small boy I used to lie awake at night, listening to the 'DONG' from the Burcombe light float, the float's bell sounding each time the vessel rolled. Our house would be easily three and a half miles from the Burcombe, which was a sandbank three miles east of the dock.

Today, more modern methods are used for lighting and bell ringing on the floats; the Burcombe Sands are still as dangerous to shipping as they were hundreds of years ago though the warning of their presence is better than it used to be. As the tide came up we would hear the rattle of anchor chains being hove up, and a bit of shouting could often be heard as well. Standing on the East Pier, with the fog getting thicker, the fog horn on the pier would seem to be working over-time. The lock gate man stood near me with his large pole, which had a line and bag attached. This was swung aboard the first vessel to enter the lock pits, the papers from the section tug were put into it and brought ashore this way to let the dock staff and telegraph know how many ships were to come to dock and what fish they had to land. More people would by now be on the pier, straining their eyes for the first vessel, wondering who it was going to be–from Iceland, the Faroes, the White Sea or the North Sea?

Then, when the sound of the ships' sirens had long gone, the crews would find their ways home in the fog after berthing their ships; the lock gates would be closed and the tide ebbing.

To my left I would hear the sound of the mud dredger working, the screeching of the chain buckets as they filled with their spoil. Perhaps with the fog still persisting, I would hear curlews crying to their mates and they seemed to be coming in one at a time. They knew the flats would be uncovered and they could get their beaks into the mud and find plenty of small worms there to eat. Stints, sand-pipers, redshank, perhaps a small gaggle of geese would come in then; also the shelduck. Sometimes the sound of a large vessel's siren would echo across the Humber. It must have come from Immingham, bound for Australia, maybe. I would not be able see it.

When the dredger had stopped dredging I would hear its

main engines working, taking its mud to be emptied on the Burcombe; then getting back into the Royal Dock basin before the tide fell too low. Tying up to the West Pier, the crew would leave the watch aboard, with the rest going home until the work started again. A never ending job, day after day, year after year, the mud must never be allowed to fill the entrance to the docks.

It was very lonely then on this pier. Packing my rod and reel, and tidying my basket up, I would decide to try another spot the next week. I had had a lousy day. Throwing my lugworms into the sea I knew that I should be digging again later, fog or fine.

Fishing was often done with handlines, not rods. Dozens of kids would fish from the Fuller Street bridge throwing the weights by hand as far as they could, giving a swing or two round and above their heads then letting go, hoping the hook was out far enough to catch a fish. Many fish were caught only a few yards out from the beach.

Suggitt's Lane was the swimming area. Some of the kids could not afford to buy a swimming costume so they had to enter the water very quickly, hoping no one saw them. Some of the boys and girls swam a long way out, and back again from Suggitts Lane.

At low water we could see the mussel beds off shore. They have long since gone. Probably the gales in latter years have helped to destroy them: nor has the oil and filth from the larger vessels helped to preserve either them or the cockles, which I have seen at North Point, black with oil. I suppose in years to come, someone with a bit of common sense will have the coast cleaned.

*   *   *   *   *   *

When I was about ten years of age, we talked to some lads who had walked to the water's edge off the Cleethorpes Pier. The spring tides went out nearly two miles–it was a long walk

8.

back, sometimes making us hurry back to the beach, as the tide starts to overtake very fast and if a fog should come in quickly it could be dangerous. So, when we did go out to the tide edge, we always dragged something on the sand as a marker, so that we could trace our way back in fog.

Some of the bigger lads who had walked to the tide edge off Cleethorpes pier told us they had been drinking clear water from a pool near to the tide edge. This was when the spring tides took the water back a great distance. Several times I heard of this fresh water but I never ventured out that far.

I remember being stranded on a bank once; luckily someone with a boat came to our rescue. Later we had a boat, which Tideswell the butcher had bought, in Tetney Creek. One day we left Tetney Lock for a wild-fowling day out; but the tide was running too strongly for us to hold with our anchor. We finished up off Spurn Point, the tide bringing us back to Tetney Lock gates in the dark around midnight. Jumping out of the boat onto the bank we sank up to our waists in mud. We managed to help each other up the bank, left the boat, and made our way home. We had been so frightened by the experience that we abandoned the boat and never went back there again.

Years later, when I was at sea, I was talking to our cook on board one of the T.C. and F. Moss boats. He lived on the Tetney Marshes in a small old house, and he told me he had once found a boat, with sails intact, and had thought that the crew must have drowned as no one ever came back for it so he had used it for himself. I think it was the one that we had abandoned!

We did have one more try, off Cleethorpes, in attempting to launch a boat as the tide came in, instead of waiting for the high tide. Rowing the boat over the bank, a sea came over the top of us, sinking us in seconds. We were a quarter of a mile from the shore and the three of us had to swim back to the beach. I could swim, but still had to be helped by my friend who was bigger and a more powerful swimmer than I was. No more boats for me.

In 1928 I was twelve years of age. My only parent and family was my mother and we lived not far from the Clee Sands. That year the Prince of Wales visited Grimsby to open the Corporation Bridge. Charles and I, with Doris our guardian, stood and watched with hundreds of other people. Leaving the bridge, the Prince looked over some of our steam trawlers. One of these was the old *Riano*–one of the sixty-two vessels owned by the Sleights. The *Riano* was the first vessel on which I went to sea whilst it was fishing. My friend, Jock MacKenzie, a wee Aberdonian, took us with him for a pleasure trip. I remember watching the men working on board during the trip, but most of the time I sat in the engine room, with Jock, sea sick and wishing I had not gone along. I must have lost a bit of weight in the six or seven days that the trip lasted because I remember mother saying my clothes were too big for me to wear

Nevertheless the next summer I had another 'pleasure' trip in the *S.T. Rononia,* one from the Bacons' firm. Leaving the Grimsby docks, I felt very low. I did not know any of the crew, the skipper having been asked to take me for a trip as I was on holiday from school. I believe many more school lads did the same in those days.

The galley's smell made me feel sick, and the warm engine room air did the same. Eating was a problem. A ship's biscuit was a favourite treatment for sea sickness. It was a large water biscuit, big as a pudding plate, and was always among the ship's stores. As I sat on the wheelhouse floor munching one of these my stomach felt as though someone was pulling the inside out. I was glad to get back to school, playing with my pals again.

My belief is that nothing in the world is worse than being sea sick. They called it a pleasure trip; not much pleasure for me, wishing at times, whilst rolling about being sick, that I could die.

CHAPTER 2

TIDE JUMP

THE STEAM TRAWLER *BALMORAL*–GY 1001

MY MOTHER–WHO WAS MY ONLY KNOWN RELATIVE–died in 1933. I went to lodge for a while with Mr. and Mrs. Vincent in Bedford Street, for five shillings per week. At that time I was working for a butcher, Arthur Tideswell, who had a shop opposite the Mariners' Rest, which was a fishhouse in those days.

Having a day off from work–butchers did not open on Mondays except for cleaning down–my friend Jack Haddock asked me to go for a walk on the docks with him. We were near the old lock gates, looking down at a trawler blowing steam off from the funnel pipe when the skipper, Johnny Vincent,. looked up at us and asked if either of us wanted to go to sea for a trip. The name on the bow was *Balmoral* GY 1001. It was from the Queens' firm.

To sea! I said to my mate: 'Do you want to go?' He replied that he had to go home. The skipper said the gates would close in ten minutes' time and one of his crew had trouble at home and could not sail.

I told him, jokingly really, that I would have gone with them but my gear was on another ship, hoping that would satisfy him. He told me that if I went he would lend me some sea clothes: he wanted to get to sea.

I found myself going aboard the ship, moving out from the quay side and out into the River Humber and realising there was no turning back now.

That was the beginning of my sea career–a wasted life? I worked hard, earned very little money, but I saw many things that I would never have seen ashore; which you will read about.

It was a very cold February day, calm and quiet, in 1933 or '34. The crew were casting the mooring ropes off the bollards whilst the vessel was slowly moving out of the lock-pits. I shouted to my friend, Jack Haddock, to tell my landlady that I had gone to sea and the name of the firm with which I had sailed.

The deck hands did not like me coming aboard, saying just ten more minutes and the gates would have been shut, and, being a man short, they would have had extra time in dock. However, going down the river, I had to sign the log book the skipper brought from his berth. Then the crew showed me how to stow the deck gear, so it did not roll about. I did what I was asked to do and tried my best to do the work that the man left on shore would have done.

The smell from the engine room and galley made me feel sick. I tried to resist this feeling by stowing the ropes and baskets and fixing the deck pounds in place. Then I had to go on the bridge, as the mate had put me in his first watch.

The mate steered for a long time until, wanting a rest, he told me to take over the wheel. The wheel was higher than I was, so standing on a wooden floor board I was taught how to steer and read the compass. After four hours on the wheel I began to feel my sea legs. The steering got better, the sea sickness went off, and I was ready for work.

Steaming somewhere down southerly from the River Humber, we fished for Dover soles. The first haul was very good, I heard the skipper say.

The crew lent me a knife and showed me how to gut the fish. I was very slow doing this, so I was given the job to wash and pair the soles. We had a wooden tub into which the donkey hose pipe was put; a knock on the side of the ship's casing indicated to the engineer on watch to start the donkey pump and pump salt water from the sea into the tub.

When the tub was half full of soles they had to be washed thoroughly, so I put my foot into the tub and booted the soles around until they were clean. After the blood had been drained from the fish we put them to bed. As they laid the fish in pairs onto the ice in the pounds the crew said that they were looked after better than gold bullion in the banks.

I did not know any of the crew and the sea gear I had been lent was not in the best of condition. One boot had a hole in the foot and my oil frock had many small tears on it. I just prayed it did not blow hard or rain during my sea voyage.

Net mending became a problem. The seaman whom I jad replaced knew how to mend the net, so it now took twice the time to get the trawl mended. I had to hold the net up for the mate or skipper, so that they could mend the holes which had been caused by wrecks on the sea bed. I was shown how to fill the wooden needles used for mending with tarry twine, the balls of hemp twine being dipped in tar along with the nets. They believed it lasted longer that way. We had large slabs of grease with which to rub the needles filled with twine: they slipped through the meshes easier. After the mending was done we tidied up the deck and stowed the trawl. If we tore the net and it took too long to mend we had to change sides. We had to do this drill several times, changing from port to starboard and vice versa. With so little rest, when we did go below for an hour's sleep and come out of the forecastle hoodway to haul the net in, we were so tired we did not know which side of the ship to go to. I remember one time young Ginger untying the quarter rope off the door where we were <u>not</u> working and taking it to the winch, still fast asleep.

The cook of the *S.T. Balmoral,* Sy–for Simon–asked me to draw some sea water from over the ship's side. He gave me a small bucket with a line attached to the handle. Throwing this bucket over the side to fill it with water was not as easy as I thought. The ship, moving through the water, took the bucket past the stern before I could fill it up, very nearly taking me off balance. I had to throw the bucket well forward, then by the time it was abreast of me I pulled it up full of water.

Sy asked me to fill the beef cask up with sea water, which, like most ships was carried lashed down on top of the galley.

He put a handful of salt-petre and two large blocks of salt in the cask, then some joints of beef. Also mutton, pork, and even sausages went in. The wooden cask had a lid on top. Half of it lifted up on hinges and a small hasp and lock was attached. The rolling of the ship kept the meat moving about in the cask, the salt keeping it fresh for weeks on end: some of the joints were taken home by the crew when a new stock came aboard.

Whilst I worked on deck, the crew taught me to gut different kinds of fish, how to wash them, and how to fill the wooden needles with tarry twine. Various jobs that I did made my hands very sore, small cuts appeared from touching spikey wires, and I would often cut myself trying to gut the fish; the salt water would open the cuts, the pain becoming unbearable at times. We had no gloves to put on, the crew did not wear any. My palms were soon twice the thickness they had been when I had come aboard.

I felt lonely and wished I had not seen the docks. The crew became more cussed with me, having to explain every little job to me that I had to do.

The weather got worse, the wind was blowing, and each man had his own work to do, there being just enough crew to manage the jobs to be done. The skipper came off the bridge, shouting and cursing: 'Fasten that down. Do this. Do that. Don't do that.' I was called everything from a pig to a dog for not knowing my work.

My hands were burning with pain. I showed them to the skipper, who told me to piss on them and the pain would go. 'That's all the medical treatment there is for sore hands out here,' he said.

I did not know the names the crew had for different parts of the ship nor the names they had for various bits of working gear and it took me a long while to remember them all.

The mate told me to ask the cook what jobs he wanted me to do during the night watch. I was told to keep the galley fire going, clean the ashes out, wash the dirty pots and keep the galley clean for him to start work early in the morning. Some cooks were up early to clean fish for breakfast not finishing until after tea at 7.00 p.m.

The cook on this vessel, Sy, was a very good cook. He particularly looked after the skipper's wants and had some perks as a consequence. Taking dinner to the skipper on the bridge was one of his jobs.

He baked bread, cakes, plum duff, and jam roll. If he wanted any little job doing the crew saw it was done for him. I made the tea, and was told to keep the tea pot going all the time that I was on watch. I have since sailed with many cooks, some disabled, two one-legged cooks, some dark coloured. Very seldom did I hear of a dirty cook.

When the crew were shooting the trawl, I had to stand clear and watch. Later the mate would explain the job to me, so that I didn't get hurt. It was a dangerous job, shooting and hauling the gear. Two thick hawsers ran from the winch drums through the deck rollers and through the gallows fore and aft. The mate told me many fishermen had been maimed or killed by climbing over the hawsers while they were being paid away off the winch. The warps, being marked, told the mate when to apply the brakes. I had to help put the messenger hook over the fore warp, letting it slide down the warp. We heaved on the messenger wire until the hook picked both wires up, whilst the third hand waited to put a large heavy block round them, then an iron pin was put through the locking device before slacking off the messenger wire. The messenger hook and wire were so called because they take the message of getting the warps together to avoid the propeller.

Both warps were now blocked, so the ship could be steered properly and none of the fishing gear could interfere with the propeller. The otter doors, now on the sea bed, kept the trawl open, one door being made to sweep to starboard and the other to port. The weight of these doors was half a ton. They had large iron shoes from one end to the other which bounced off rocks, stones and shells, sometimes sticking in the mud and

15.

stopping the ship, then the warps would have to be heaved up in the block to clear them.

When we moved to a different fishing ground we hung the doors on large chains, outboard on the gallows, and when we were ready to haul our gear, the deck hand on watch would stand by aft with a heavy hammer in his hands. As soon as the skipper had the ship in position for hauling, he would shout, 'Knockout!' The deckhand, being ready, would pull the pin out and hit the upper part of the block, parting the two warps to be heaved back on to the winch.

For the first day or two, I was unable to stand or walk on deck properly. My legs got tired, wobbling about and I had to grab and hold on to anything I could find to steady myself from falling overboard. The freeboard (which is the height of the rail above the deck) on the ships was only just above my knees.

Each man had his own work to do, the mate telling me to do this, do that. I had to ask the other decky to explain what was wanted of me, and somehow got away with it. I had had to learn to splice knots, gut and wash fish, steer the ship, make the tea, read the lead line, sling the lead (which weighed seven to ten pounds) with the end hollowed out and filled with grease. This lead line was dropped many times during the trip. The skipper knows his position by whatever the lead line tells him The line is marked in fathoms which gives the depth at that point and, after being dropped on the sea bed, the sand, mud and stones would stick into the grease at the bottom of the lead. The nearest mark to the surface of the water was called to the skipper who had a look and a feel at the lead's bottom and would mutter to himself and then plot his position on the chart.

Pulling this lead line in frequently while fishing was a problem. The lead and line had to be taken forward while towing the gear then swung and cast as far forward as possible, letting it go until you could feel that it had hit the bottom and running aft at the same time so that the line was vertical to get the depth of the water.. If nothing was shown on the grease at the bottom the lead had to be dropped again until the skipper was satisfied that he had a good reading. Pulling this lead and line up many times a day made my hands sore and swollen but that didn't get any sympathy from the rest of the crew. They just repeated the advice that the skipper had given to me 'to piss on them'.

I remember when the skipper told me to clean the fishing lights, fill them with paraffin and haul them up to the top of the foremast. 'It's getting dark now and I need them up,' he said. To do this I had to lie on the deck to pull the halyards with my feet touching the bottom of the mast. Very large lanterns they were, made of copper and brass, and heavy too. The light had three colours on the front, red, white and green.

The ship rolled and tossed about but at last I got the light to the top of the mast. Alas, the lantern had several times hit the mast going up and put the light out. I had to repeat the process time and time again before I got the hang of it. Then the all round light had to be hauled up just underneath the triple light. This had a white light showing all round the horizon.

During the night the wind dropped. I felt a little better, the crew were not so cussed and the urine must have been doing my hands a lot of good and the pain was easing off.

The skipper and mate took note of the fish we had caught.

To work on the deck at night was mostly guess-work. No wonder so many accidents happened on board these ships. We had a small can, shaped like a watering can, with a small spout into which a piece of waste rag had been pushed and the can filled with paraffin, This was hung on the gallows bar near the foreward starboard pound. Lighting this with a match it would last many hours burning and give some light, There were two more gas lanterns hung in the centre of the fish pounds just to light the pounds.

We fastened a wire from the foremast to the bridge and a small bore pipe travelled to the engine room. The engineers had a contraption into which they put carbide and with water dripping into it. This gave off an inflammable gas (acetylene, as was used in the early bicycle lamps) which was led to the cabin, galley, compass binnacle and the two deck lights. The burners had to be pricked out with a piece of thin wire and cleaned every day. We had lots of trouble when the engineers had no time to clean this, and we had to leave the fish in baskets during the darkness, the watch deckhand gutting it as daylight appeared, the catch being washed and iced away by the crew later.

We had to pull the trawl aboard with our bare hands, the tarry net sticking like glue to our fingers. My hands became thick and strong. Some skippers used chains from door to door dragging under the sea bed and making the fish swim upwards into the net. As many as five of these 'tickler chains' were used at once, making it hard work. Many of these chains broke on wrecks, having to be mended with false links.

After we had been at sea a day or two I needed to use the toilet. Asking the mate, he explained to me that there had been no toilet for twenty years or more. The place that had been the toilet was now used for bobbins, ropes, wires, twine etc., He and the crew used the ship's rail, holding on to the gallows bar, at whichever part of the ship was preferred: starboard foreward, starboard aft, port foreward or port aft, depending on which was the lee side, that was away from the wind. He told me that I could ask the engineer if I could use the stokehold for a toilet. Sometimes the engineer would let me, if in a good mood and not cleaning a fire. But he did not like the smell, and often refused permission. During fine weather we could use the scuppers but you might get a wetting as the ship rolled. I preferred the ship's rail, foreward or aft, clinging onto the gallows bar.

Breakfast was in two shifts: the first sitting was 6.00–6.30 a.m. and the second 6.30–7.00 a.m. Dinner was 12.00 noon–12.30 p.m. and 12.30 to 1.00 p.m. Tea was 6.00–6.30 p.m. and 6.30–7.00 p.m..

18.

During the night, whilst fishing, we would toast cheese with bread in the oven. Maybe a herring, if caught, would be toasted on the ash grate, or a stray mullet on the hot coals.

All the small fish would be saved for the cook, taken aft and hung on the lifeboat's rollocks in a basket. If the crew had time during the night it would be cleaned for the cook. We would have fish every morning for breakfast; fish was also served for tea, but never was fish cooked for dinner unless a longer sea trip than planned was necessary, then maybe we'd have a cod cooked in the oven.

The longest period during which I had three meals a day of fish was about fourteen days. A new cook had used all the food up too quickly so, as we were making a long trip, we had to eat more fish.

During the voyage home from the fishing grounds we had to stow the nets. The third mate would make a large 'sausage' with his cod ends, all nicely cleaned of any fish or weed. He would heave them tight to the top of the gallows' bar and make them fast, the trawl and bobbins neatly stowed in the ship's side. Both sides had to be done as we had two trawls.

All loose gear and baskets were washed and put down the forehold. The pound boards were washed and stowed away for the next trip and the hatches were battened down with tarpaulins and iron bars. Wooden wedges were used to tighten the iron bars into the hatch sides. The wedges were always put into their sockets from forward to aft, as the sea coming aboard would wash them out if put the other way; which has been done many times. This was one reason why a good mate would always see that this battening down done properly.

The steaming lights had to be lit, the fishing lights hauled down and steaming light pulled to the top of the foremast. Side lights, port and starboard, were swung out on the veranda, and a small paraffin lantern fastened aft, where it could be seen by following vessels.

The decks were hosed down, the wheelhouse and fo'c's'le

cleaned, the cook cleaning the galley with the stove being blackleaded and looking very nice. He also cleaned the cabin, polishing the brass lantern that swung in the centre of the table from the deck head.

Approaching Spurn Light Vessel, the mate asked me to pull the log line in and read the mileage on it. I had to untie the log line, letting the end go into the sea, reversing the line to take the turns out, then pull it in again, coiling it in nice round loops ready to be used on the following trip. The log line is a piece of equipment used to measure distance travelled through the water, It works rather like a mileometer on a car or bicycle with a cable being turned by a 'propeller' like device on the end of a cable as the vessel passes through the water.

Approaching the River Humber there were several light vessels. We passed the Dowsing L.V., the Humber L.V., the Spurn L.V, which was painted black (now a monument in Hull Marina). Passing Spurn Point on the starboard bow during daylight, the Grimsby Dock Tower would be in view. We passed the two old forts built during the 1914-18 war, until we came to the Burcombe Lightbuoy, where we dropped anchor, about three miles from the docks, looking west.

It was low tide so we had to wait several hours before the tide came up sufficiently to allow the lock pit gates to open and the trawlers into the dock.

So we had plenty of time to wash ourselves down, before going ashore.

There was a routine for this too. The trimmer took a bucket of water from the ship's galley tin and washed down in the fo'c'sle, the cook washed down in his cabin after taking the skipper a bucket of hot water to his cabin on the bridge; he washed down there. The engineer told me I could wash down behind the engines; taking some water in an old carbide tin out of the distilled water tank I had a good strip wash and freshened myself up. We were all very tired but seemed to liven up coming home. Coming on deck in my shore clothes seemed very queer after having heavy sea gear on for the previous ten days. Taking the anchor watch, I looked through the ship's binoculars at the dock tower, and at the signals which were pulled up by the dock gatemen. After the tide had risen so many feet a black ball could be seen to appear on a yard-arm on Fish Dock Island. After two black balls went up it was time to heave the anchor up and be ready to enter the lock. At three black balls the gates were opened.

We had been the first vessel to drop anchor this tide. The section tug, which was then *The Condor*, with GY on the stern, came alongside. The skipper of the tug told our skipper to hoist a small blue flag foreward, to indicate we were the leader of No. 1 section. There were ten ships in each of Nos. 1, 2, 3, 4 and 5 sections; that would be fifty vessels. During the night white lanterns were used instead of black balls, indicating how much water there was in the lock pits. These signals were pulled up in all weathers.

The gale signal was a cone, upright for a north gale, cone nose down for a south gale, on the Dock Tower.

When the section tug *Condor* saw the signal for the gates opening, its whistle gave one long blast, to let the other ships know we were on the move towards the dock, the other vessels following.

Sometimes skippers tried to go into the dock before their turn. They would be reported to the Dock Master who then sent a letter of warning to them. This practise soon stopped, all taking their proper turns.

Coming into the dock, the trimmer stayed in the stern, a rope fender in his hands to be put between the ship's side and the lock pit wall if needed. Sometimes the tide was so fast it took the vessel onto the wall. The mate stood forward in the bows, keeping a lookout, letting the skipper know where to berth the ship, with the two deckhands holding their fenders one either side of the ship.

Coming into No.1 Dock, near the lock pits, we moored on

the iron bollards. Ropes out, the skipper rang the telegraph several times to let the engineer know he was finished with engines. Passing the sea bags ashore, the crew started to leave the ship. The mate came over to me to say I had got the sack. He wanted his own man back again. He would put a word in for me to the ships' runner to see I was given another ship.

I had to help with the landing next morning at 5.00 a.m. We made a very good trip, the skipper saying I had been lucky to him, it was the best trip he had made.

Leaving the ship after it had been moored, I was met by Skipper Joe Marlow, whose son Charles had been my school pal. He was No.1 Tug in Grimsby Docks, towing ships to the coal jetty, ice quay and so on as required. He lived with his family in Imperial Avenue, Cleethorpes, and told me Jack Haddock had gone to his house, letting them know I had gone to sea; would I like to lodge with them? Mrs. Marlow became my landlady from then on until I married in 1937.

CHAPTER 3

FROM ASHORE TO 'NEW TO THE GAME'

HAVING HAD A BATH AND A GOOD SLEEP, I caught the tram to the Lincoln Arms public house, Riby Square, getting on the tram at the Imperial Hotel, Cleethorpes; the fare then being 2d (tuppence, or two old pence). My landlady had been to Queens' office for my pay, £1–18s–6d, and to which would be added 2d in the £ 'poundage' (or bonus). My lodgings then were 15/- (fifteen shillings) per week, in or out of dock.

'Weaver to Wearer' had opened a shop in Freeman Street. So I went there and had a suit made-to-measure for thirty shillings. Near the White Swan public house, opposite to where the Humber Hotel now stands, was a boot factory where I had a pair of black patent leather shoes made, with bulldog toe effect, for five shillings.

The Grimsby and Danish fishermen were always dressed in nice suits, many handmade by Jewish tailors who each knew who had made a suit. When standing near a tailor he would look at the stitching and know who had made it for you.

After a few days ashore, I had a walk down to the docks again. There were hundreds of fishermen on the docks. Ten thousand fishermen could not be at sea all at once: some were signing on the dole, and some were fitting out, waiting for repairs to be done to their ships. Queens' firm, T. Robinson, Atlas, T.C. & F. Moss, G.F. Sleight, Taylors, Crampins, Butts, Bannisters, Bacons, Littles, H. Franklins, were just a few of the firms on the docks where crowds of fishermen waited for work. By about 11.30 a.m. the docks would be clear of fishermen, many having gone home until the next day, others going into their local clubs or pubs.

Some men would wait at Riby Square for the fishermen who had landed and gone down to the dock for their poundage,

23.

hoping for a treat from them. Sometimes the policeman on point duty at Riby Square would ask them to move off as they were stopping shoppers from walking on the pavement.

I used to have a meal and then go back on the dock around 2.00 p.m. to see if a job had turned up. I knew I stood little chance of a job with a hundred or so fishermen all looking for work during the early hours, but it came into my mind that if a job did turn up and I was around I stood a better chance of getting it when the married crewmen had gone home. Some would-be crewmen for the best ship's crews dropped a few shillings to the runners who could tell them of a berth on a good earning vessel; but if the skipper heard of it that man was quickly sacked.

E. Bacon's ships' runner asked me to see him and promised me a job. Meanwhile, passing Doughty's office, I was asked to sign on the *S.T. River Witham* for a trip, which suited me better as I could learn a little more about the job.

I had to buy a donkey's breakfast (a straw bed) from Dobby's Stores for 5/-, a new oil frock for 10/-, and a new knife for 1/-. I did not smoke, so I wasn't worried about fags. During my time going to and from Dobby's Stores, which was on the corner of Cross Street, I had to go across the swing bridge which spanned the cutting on the dock. On one journey I had to wait until the largest trawler afloat at that time passed through the cutting. This was the *William Grant*, later to be renamed *Gatooma*. She left Grimsby at a later date (in 1938) for Italy.

I was ready for my second trip to the North Sea but there would be several more before venturing to the northern fishing grounds in about late 1934.

After I had returned from that trip, and when I had spent my money and broken in my new clothes I went to look for another ship. I had heard that Harold Moss, a 'ship's husband' for T.C. & F. Moss, Fish Dock Road, Grimsby, was looking for deck hands. Harold Moss was the brother of Tom, Charles, and Fred

Moss, who owned several steam trawlers.

Tom Moss was a magistrate at Grimsby County Court, and a very strict man. He sat behind his desk in his office on the docks, and looked at you over the tops of his glasses. Billy Moss, his son, was cashier, and Harold signed you on the ship.

Harold was known as the Stone Wall Ghost. He was always on the lookout for the kind of men he could trust to be on time when the ships were ready to sail, and no one did the job better than him. He always saw that the ships had coal, water, ice, and food aboard ready for sea: then the crew. The ships were very old and I had heard that some of the crew were too. It was common in that firm that some of the crews had been with one ship for fifteen or twenty years

I signed on the *S.T. Diamond* built in the year 1894, sister ship to the *Emerald* built in the same year. I bought another donkey's breakfast, this time from Colbridge's Stores, and Mrs. Marlow, my landlady, supplied my blanket.

Going on board I met old Joe, the trimmer. He was putting his sea gear on ready to get the ship's pound boards and to stow any loose gear lying about the deck. The noise from the trawlers leaving the quay side was awful. There must have been twenty or thirty ships with engines going astern at the same time and, in the middle of the dock, those leaving the lock pits all seemed to be blowing their whistles at the same time. 'Cock a Doodle Doo', the big ships would blow as they left the docks. When we left the dock, there was just one large black cloud from all the ships that had left with smoke pouring from their funnels, the engines had been making steam to run the winches for hawsers and anchor cable, as well as the engines. Even the whistle of the siren was steam which of course we had to sound during foggy weather to let any other ships know we were in their vicinity.

We used to blow the whistle to passing trawlers, coming home, and when we left the docks we blew a 'Cock a Doodle Doo' several times. The people in the streets of Grimsby always knew it was tide time, hearing this noise.

This being only my third fishing trip to sea I still had a lot to learn, being what was called a 'rooky'. The mate kept his eye on the compass whilst I did the steering, the skipper having set the course before he turned in. As we steamed easterly the mate told me the cargo boats going north-west were in the first shipping lane: we would pass the second shipping lane later. We passed the Humber Light Vessel and one of the keepers give us a wave with his big cap. We carried on until we came to the Outer Dowsing L.V., when the mate told the skipper, who gave him a fresh course, the mate told me to turn the wheel to port and gave me the course to steer, which to my amazement I managed first time. The weather was cold but calm.

Then the mate took the wheel whilst I fetched two mugs of tea from the galley, the smell from the throbbing engines making me feel sea sick. I lost half the tea climbing the iron stairs to the bridge and had to go back to the galley for more.

The galley was not very big with just enough room to walk in front of the large stove which the cook kept clean and a good fire going all day. It had a very big oven and on the right side there was a huge ship's pan: it was a square one with hot water always in it. The watch took over at night time, making the tea for the following watch.

After steaming for a few hours the skipper came on the bridge and blew down a voice pipe to the engine room, telling the engineer on the watch to let some of his steam go down as he wanted to stop the ship for a sounding. The engineer would ring the telegraph to let the skipper know his steam was down ready to stop ship when required.

After I had brought the skipper a pot of tea, he rang the telegraph and stopped the ship, bringing the wind, which was light at the time, onto the starboard side. Remember this was in the 1930's. We had no navigational aids like today; the only things to navigate with were the sextant, the hand lead line for depth of water, the log line for distance travelled, and the compass. The older and experienced men could read the lead like reading a book. Some of the skippers couldn't read and write but they could read the lead line and compass alright. After I had greased the lead and pulled it up the skipper shouted: 'How many fathoms?' I said: 'By the mark, seventeen fathoms and rough sand on the bottom'. He replied to the mate: 'Steer so-and-so for half an hour and then we'll shoot the trawl away. Call all hands to have a drink, and get the trawl boards outside of the gallows.' This was all done, and the lead again had to be used, fine sand at twenty-one fathoms. We shot the gear away for the first time on this, my second, trip.

We had to haul up the fishing lights which the trimmers had ready. During the first fishing watch I had to fix the deck pound boards into place for the catch to go in, take my turn on the wheel whilst the mate or third hand had his meal–and so it went on . . . and on. It was the same thing all the time, haul, gut fish, wash fish, the mate putting the fish away with the trimmer helping him. When the net became torn it had to be repaired. The skipper, mate, and third hand got mending it, the trimmer filling the wooden needles with tarry twine. Nylon was NOT on the menu then. I could not mend and had to hold the net up for the menders. A good decky could mend nets so I took notice how and what had to be done. Going to nautical school and learning to mend was quite different; there it was mending nice clean netting laid out to work on but on a ship, rolling and tossing, the net full of weed and in knots, with water coming over the ship's rail, was no easy task. You had to be good to be a net mender at sea.

The job I had when hauling the net in was with the mate on the winch with each of us holding a brake to heave the large otter boards in first, then the bobbins (small cork floats) and then all hands pulling in the net; the bag of fish going forward and the trimmer pulling on a Jilson wire (a single wire with a hook on it which was 'out of the way' on the opposite side to the fishing side and which was through a roller on the foremast. Up came the bag into the forward pounds where the third hand was waiting to open the special knot he had made at the bottom of the cod ends (the bottom of the net which was opened to release the catch when it was placed for the catch to be emptied in the required place) the fish teeming in all four pounds.

'A good haul,' says the skipper, 'we'll put a dan bouy (a marker buoy with a tall pole above the water which could then be seen from a distance) down to mark our position, so we don't drift away from the ground where the fish are.' (Today there is no need for a dan buoy, the instruments they have tell them where they are and even the time of day.) The dan buoys were kept in the rigging, large poles thirty feet long that had a large pack of cork which the pole went through three quarters of the way up; it had a heavy weight on the bottom with a small anchor and forty fathoms of small wire. We heaved this over the side and the engineer came up with a light to fasten onto the buoy so that we could see it in the dark. The light was a carbide contraption and had to be cleaned every day. There was a small burner which the engineer pricked out every day with a small piece of wire. A flag made of a piece of red rag was on top of the pole during the day.

The engineer also had to look after the two light we hung on a wire from the wheelhouse to the foremast so that we could see the fish in the pounds at night. During bad weather these blew out many times and had to be relit time and time again.

We used the lead line again, the buoy was anchored in twenty fathoms. The skipper looked among the catch for telltale pieces of weed. Looking at them and feeling them gave him the course to the River Humber. He may not have been able to read or write but he could read the bottom of the sea and knew exactly the position his ship was in from the River Humber.

I noticed that during the day the skipper would sit on the after-rail and watch the two warps which were towing the trawl. If the warps widened he knew the water was shallowing and if they closed he knew the water was deepening, and he would tell the helmsman to steer another course more to his liking.

Ships today have instruments from which, at the press of a

button, the skipper knows the position, depth of water, whether the bottom is sand, stones or whatever, and even the time of day. I will tell you later how we knew the time, coming from the Pentland Firth.

In February at night the weather was cold. We had very little light to see the otter doors coming when we were hauling the trawl up. So we rigged a light and made it fast to the gallows bar, forward of the ship near the bow, whichever side trawl we were using. The light was a tin can shaped like a small watering can as already explained. Once lit it kept alight in all weathers: rain, wind, or snow there were no problems with it.

We didn't get a lot of sleep. We towed for four hours unless we came fast to some object, such as a large stone or maybe an old wreck at the bottom of the sea. The skipper cursed when we became fast. Sometimes not keeping in the right depth of water could take us onto wrecks or fasteners: he knew where they lay but tried to just miss them. The skipper said that sometimes if you got close to a wreck, but kept your trawl clear, you could catch a bag of cod–which at times we did.

For meal times we lost half an hour's sleep. The bigger the catch, the longer we gutted and put fish away, also losing sleep time.

During the time the trawl was shot away the mate would send the trimmer down to the fish room, to chop enough ice for the fish we had to put down from the previous haul.

After the fish was stowed, the trimmer then had to pull the ashes from the engine room. Each watch the chief engineer and second engineer pulled one fire out and cleared all the ashes from the stoke hold. Old carbide tins were used to do this job, two holes being made at the top of each tin and two hooks were lowered on rope halyards over a small wheel down the lee-side ventilator. The engineer filled the ash-buckets and the trimmer pulled them up and emptied them overboard. If the weather was bad the ashes were emptied on deck and the sea coming aboard washing them away. The ashes had to be cleared every watch, keeping the stokehold tidy. If the ashes were wet it was a hard pull up.

Every man had his job to do. The crew consisting of skipper, mate, third hand (or boatswain), two engineers, two deck hands, one trimmer and one cook; nine in all. Trawlers going to the Westerly and Faroes had two extra men to fire the ship until they started fishing, then they became deck hands and the engineers had to fire and look after the engines themselves. Larger vessels going to Iceland, Bear Island and the White Sea might have a galley boy, twelve; thirteen if the skipper had a wireless operator. Some of the skippers carried a decky wireless operator, twelve men and a galley boy. The Board of Trade allowed no more until later years.

Whilst fishing, I used to watch the different kinds of fish we caught in the net and the odd pieces of bone, etc. I picked a large piece of amber out of the pound one day. Another day I was given a piece of ambergris which would be worth quite a lot of money today. I put these in the small boat we carried aft, but I forgot all about them after coming back to Grimsby.

We fished for about ten days, the same routine every day. When we came in to dock we had to land the fish with the lumpers. It was my job to pull on the bell ropes; four ropes passing through a wheel aloft with four men pulling the baskets of fish out of the fishroom. The hatchway man swung the baskets of fish onto the landing boards, where the trimmer's job was to catch the basket and take the hooks out of the it's handles, pass them back to the hatchway man, then pull the basket of fish down the planks onto the pontoon where the lumpers took over and sorted the fish, the cod being laid out on the pontoon in scores (i.e. twenties). The fish was looked after properly in the ship and it looked as if it was still alive.

After landing, I decided to have a bath in Riby Square lavatories. It was a very smart toilet (as it would be called today), baths all white, walls all white tiled and cleaned each day by the attendants who were dedicated to their job. My bath was filled with hot water, and a clean towel and a small piece of hard soap were provided. I believe that I paid sixpence (6d.–old money).

After my bath I visited a barber, across the road from the lavatories, passing the old horse trough in the middle of the square. The horses and carts stood from the Ragland corner (the Ragland was a public house at the corner of Orwell Street) to the Police Box near Cleethorpes Road. My barber was Jack Death, and he was very quick with a razor. I sat in the chair, the bit of fluff on my face was like goose down.

He said, whilst swinging the razor near my face: 'Have you been to Iceland?' (one swipe): 'Faroes?' (another swipe): 'White Sea?' (another swipe) 'North Sea?' wiped my face with a towel and said: 'Next please'. I was out of the shop in a flash. At 11.00 a.m. I was at the Moss's office for my pay and poundage: £1-18s-6d per week, plus poundage at 2d in the £. after expenses were taken off.

After several trips as a decky, and being sacked after each trip because I could not mend the net, I was asked by Bacon's Steam Trawler runner if I would go in one of his ships. The runner, as we called them in those days, found the crews for the ships. Each firm had a runner and there were many different firms owning trawlers. In Fish Dock Road alone there were Crampins, who had trawlers lying off Greenland, Toshes, Bannisters, Bacons, Mosses, Queens' firm, Butts, Franklins and many more. I'd say around ten thousand fishermen lived in Cleethorpes and Grimsby. Many had fathers and sons going in the same ships. Many were lost at sea. The names of the ships and lost were registered in the Fishermen's Chapel in Tiverton Street, Cleethorpes; later in Duncombe Hall. Duncombe Street, Grimsby–where they are today.

Going down to the docks, I had to bring my bed out of Couldbridge's Stores, where we paid a few pence for them to store our sea gear, instead of taking it home. If we needed boots or a frock, oil frocks as we named them, and a sou'wester oil skin cap, we had to sign a form and the ship's runner would have the money stopped out of our wages. Frocks cost 10/-

apiece then, boots £2.00, a sou'wester 2/6d. It was a lot of money to spend so we had to look after our gear. Sometimes we had to take our frocks home, buy a bottle of boiled linseed oil and paint them with it to make them waterproof again, as the rain took the newness out of a frock and it became like a wet cloth hanging round your shoulders. Some of the older fishermen had leather sea boots, but rubber boots took over later.

Putting my sea gear on board in the fo'c'sle and having a yarn with the trimmer and my opposite number, the other decky, I was informed that we would be out fishing for eleven or twelve days with this skipper. I was given two or three boxes of matches and these had to last me the trip, for lighting fires, etc.

After leaving the dock, and steaming for approximately two hours, I was told to stream the log line. It was the first time I had done this on my own. I'd watched the deck hands on previous vessels do this job, and I had taken notice. A small brass clip was secured to the after rail. I put the log clock in the clip and made it fast with a small line, making the log line fast to the wheel which was attached to the clock. Then finally a fan with three blades was attached and thrown over the side. After the line had become tight I pulled on the wheel, making it spin round. The log clock was now working, and I set it, just as the light ship came abreast of us.

Every hour we would read the log clock to see how many miles per hour (knots) the ship was making through the water. (a knot is one nautical mile of 2,000 yards per hour: it is a measure of speed, not directly of distance) After we had steamed for eleven hours, with one hundred and ten miles on the clock, I was asked to pull the log line in. This had to be done by untying the knot from the wheel, pulling in the line at the same time, and letting the end of the line go back into the ship's wake again. When the fan came aboard, all the turns in the log line had gone, and I pulled the line in for the second time, coiling it neatly and easily and hanging it on the life-boat until it should be required again.

I noticed the Spurn Light Vessel was painted black. The skipper told me that it was the only black painted lightship around our coasts, the others were painted red.

Spurn Light House was painted black and white and its light revolved left-handed. Other light-houses revolved right-handed. On a very clear night I could see Flamborough Head, Withernsea, Spurn, Outer Dowsing, and Haisborough. All the looms from these lights could be seen from fifty to sixty miles away. In frosty weather, and on a clear dark night, we could see these looms clearly as we rose on a wave or swell, the lights flashing at their allotted intervals,

Chapter 4

At Sea and Ashore

I REMEMBER SAILING IN ONE OF MOSS'S TRAWLERS. The skipper was a Lowestoft man who used to be a drifter skipper in his younger days, he was then in his sixtieth year. Most of these old Lowestoft fishermen went to sea at twelve years of age. Some could not read or write, but they knew the North Sea and much of the shore line around our Isles. The herring took twelve months to circumnavigate our shores, so the Lowestoft and Yarmouth drifters were fishing away from home for nine months of the year. But from September until Christmas time the herring came in their millions to just outside their home town so the Lowestoft and Yarmouth vessels were always home for Christmas.

This story was told to me about a drifter, *Silver Dawn*, which landed its catch one morning in Yarmouth. One of its crew wanted a night at home. The man taking his place could have £2 for the night's fishing, which was a lot of money if you did not catch any herring, or he could gamble on the night's fishing: no fish, no money. He gambled on the catch instead of taking the money.

After leaving the nets drifting all night, when daylight was breaking, pulling in the nets was too much for the *Silver Dawn's* crew. The skipper had to hoist a flag and seek help from the naval fisheries vessel which kept watch on the drifters, their sailors helping to pull the nets abroad. The stand-in crewman received nearly £100 for his night's work!

Out of a hundred drifters working, maybe five would catch enough to pay the expenses for the night's work. Some won, some lost.

We had been in Lowestoft to seek shelter from a northerly gale, the first time I had experienced a gale. We'd been fishing at Smith's Knoll, outside the banks. I reckon two hundred drifters had been fishing at the same time. All had oil lamps lit on their forestays at night, the nets hanging just below the waterline, white painted bladders held their nets up like a large curtain, stretching two to three miles from the bows. The herrings, swimming fast, would catch their heads in the meshes and their gills stop them from 'reversing' or swimming any further.

We had to trawl between two drifters, the bladders we could see on either side of us. We caught some large cod and turbot, all of which were full of herrings. The deck was littered with half eaten fish after we had gutted our catch. Sometimes the Naval Protection Vessel would come close by with his loud hailer. He would ask our skipper to move out of the vicinity of the drifters but the fishery skipper, looking through his binoculars, knowing who our skipper was told him to carry on where he wanted to fish. He had known the skipper for many years and had fished with him.

FISHING OFF GERMANY 1936-7

Fishing in very cold weather on the west coast of Germany, we had a first haul and it consisted of a large bag of brown shells. To look at, they were as big as a walnut but they could be crushed between the fingers like brown biscuits. The skipper said that they were called 'Dutch farts', and we would have to move from this area because no fish ever came while the shells were here.

We moved further north and shot the trawl again. Night time came with a very cold, clear sky, and a starry night. It was my watch and in the distance to the east I could see lights, like large pencil shapes, flashing all over the sky. The next thing I saw was a white object in the light, and all the other lights became concentrated on this object. I called the skipper and he said it was a plane and the lights were searchlights scanning the sky. We had not seen anything like this before and we did not realise that it was Jerry preparing for war.

Next day we saw twelve German destroyers in line. We did not carry a wireless so we could not tell any of our other trawlers what we had seen. Anyway no other trawlers were near. During the day, while we were fishing, a plane came over and scattered silver paper over us. I picked some up off the deck but could not make head or tail of it, until later when we were at war and our planes did the same thing to the enemy, to interfere with their radio and radar (which, of course, at that time, we had not even heard about): but we had no wireless and we were left alone to fish.

We left the German coast and, coming back to the River Humber, we could see the Dowsing light flashing ninety miles away. We could see Flamborough Head light flashing, Spurn Head, the Withernsea light and Haisborough light all together. That night was cold and frosty and we could see the Aurora Borealis–the Northern Lights–flashing too.

THE COMPASS

I learnt how to box the compass: that is, to read and know it North to East and North to West, or, the right way and the left way. One skipper taught me the cobbler's compass, nail by heel and sole by welt, all round the compass. And I learnt how to mend the trawl the hard way.

My friend Fred Anson, a Hull man living in lodgings in the same street as I was, told me to wait for him coming home from the Faroes Islands, where he had gone fishing, then I could sail with him and he would teach me to splice, and so on. I stayed ashore as he was due in dock any day.

Picking up the morning paper, I was stunned to read that Fred's ship had been hit by a freak wave, on the way home off Aberdeen, and the wheelhouse and funnel had been washed overboard. Fred was lost, but the deckhand on watch with him, being in the galley making tea at the time, was O.K. The ship was brought into the Deen and repaired enough to come home to Grimsby, but there was no Fred.

I went to Hull to see his parents. His father, being an old fisherman, showed me Fred's gold watch and a framed letter from President von Hindenberg who was the German Chancellor at the time, who had sent it to Fred for helping to save a German ship's crew that had grounded on Bear Island. Fred's father gave me oil frocks and boots, and a sextant, as he had no further use for them.

I got myself another ship and sailed for the Faroes. It was one of W.W. Butt's ships. Mr. Jack Rouse was the ship's husband, and he only wanted the best fishermen and men he knew would work hard. If you were in W.W. Butt's firm you had to be good, so this was my chance. Faroe vessels, Iceland, White Sea and Bear Island ships were all in Butt's firm.

THE PUBS AND CLUBS

Whilst I was in dock I used to spend my time like the other fishermen. I liked a drink and I mostly used the public houses around Freeman Street. There were one hundred and ten beer houses in the Cleethorpes and Grimsby area, and each had the fishermen of their own district as customers. If I required to visit a friend of mine I would know where to find him. If he was in dock Jack Jones would be in the Imperial, Amos Hubbard would be in the Clee Park, and so on. Christmas time found most fishermen at home. The Grimsby football team always played at home on Christmas Day, the club having the privilege to suit the fishermen's wishes. Some ships were at sea fishing and a Light Vessel crew were always at sea at Christmas and New Year, like the lighthouse keeper and the dock gate men who had to attend the lock gates, holidays or not.

Myself, I had no relatives in Grimsby. So I had a pint whenever I wished.

Mr friend, a Danish fisherman, Ogga Neilson, of Frederickshaven, Denmark, came to fish out of Grimsby with many more fishermen, fishing until the end of October. Then they sailed home again for the winter, returning after catching a trip in the spring time.

I remember many Danish seine netters going home for the winter and getting caught in a gale of wind that had got up very quickly while they were on the Dogger Bank. One of my friends was holding the rigging when the ship he was in turned right over. He put his foot in the ropes and went underneath the water, then came up again, the mate having had the presence of mind to cut the sail rope, which would have been under the water and stopped the ship righting itself. They made it back to Denmark minus the cook, with whom I had been out shopping to buy his family Christmas presents.

A very sad time that was. Many ships and crews were lost, among them several friends of mine. Ogga's brother, Peter, was lost. Ogga, today, is the only one of seven brothers left. He lives at Frederickshaven with his family. Occasionally I write to him and he writes back, half the letter is in Danish and the other half English, but I understand. I believe his mother still lives, having had twelve children, the five girls still living. Ogga used to fish at Iceland from Denmark in the 1930s in very small seine netters.

* * * * *

Coming off the docks, during drinking hours, we first called at the Lord Ragland hotel in Riby Square, at the corner of Orwell Street, opposite the Seamen's Mission.

Trixie was the barmaid. Our beer was on the counter before we had ordered it, money or no money. She knew that when we made a trip the money we owed would be paid back or more.

The Kent Arms still stands in Kent Street, the old Kent

having been knocked down and rebuilt after a few bombs fell around it during the war. Burt's, the grocers, ground their own coffee in Cleethorpes Road, so the drunks knew where they were by the smell. That is not there any more.

On Kent Street corner was Burgon's bacon and egg shop, renowned for smoked bacon and different cheeses that could be smelled from far away.

Going down Freeman Street, towards the market, there was the smell of paraffin burning from the lamps each stall had hung up on their top bars. The beer pubs had their doors wide open and the smell of the beer was there. Cow-heels and pigs' trotters made a good meal with the beer, people going into one pub, then another, eating the trotters as they went. Beer was 6d a pint, trotters 2d each, cow-heels 6d; they made a smashing meal.

Old George Earl had a pub in Albert Street, the Freemasons' Arms. Mrs. Bates had the White Bear opposite on Thesigar Street and Albert Street corner, and the Crown and Anchor was on Albert Street and Freeman Street corner: there were The Robin, Globe, Smokers, Queens, Dogger Bank, Prince of Wales, Locomotive, Crown and Buckle, and many many more in just a small area. The ale was good and strong, 6d a pint, and all made a living.

A very old pal of mine told me a story about his father who was skipper of a Grimsby smack. The smack belonged to W. Butt's firm, which also owned three pubs in Grimsby: the White Swan, Victor Street and Cleethorpes Road, the Gloucester Arms in Albert Street, and the Havelock in Kent Street and Bridge Street. During fitting out times, the skippers had to work in the pubs if they wanted any wages, so my friend's father was told to serve in the bar at the Gloucester Arms Hotel. While he was serving there, his crew sent a message that they were drinking in the Mariner's Compass, opposite the Gloucester Arms, and the message said they had no money left. The skipper took money from the till and went across the road to where his crew were and joined them with their drinking. I suppose some time later the money was repaid from his settlings.

My friend also told me about a stone he brought home from sea and put on a cistern in his back yard, to stop small children falling down it.

The old Oxford cinema became the Oky dance hall where young fishermen went for a night's frolic. The old Rialto was another haunt we visited for entertainment but the Gaiety dance hall was a bigger and nicer place to visit.

Betty Blood's café in Victoria Street–who remembers that?

During one of my visits to the Gloucester Arms I heard a woman singing. You could have heard a pin drop, it was so quiet. I remembered a few words Annie Wilcox sang that night.

> *Just like a fool in a story, without you I cannot live,*
> *Just like a fool I still love you, can't you live and forgive,*
> *In the Heart of a fool that was broken*
> *Just like a ship at sea.*
> *There's a story old, that's never been told,*
> *Of a wreck you made of me.*
> *Like a baby that breaks all its playthings*
> *You broke my heart, that is true.*
> *Though you've been untrue there's a prayer left for you*
> *Deep in the heart of a fool.*

Many more songs she sang in pubs and clubs.

> *Just an old-fashioned trawler, with an old-fashioned crew*
> *And the skipper says 'Welcome' to you,*

was one of her favourite songs.

* * * * *

It was always said that oil and salt water do not mix; and

they did not mix in Grimsby.

The engineers had their own club in Cleethorpes Road, and their own Union in Orwell Street. If you were in a public house you would find the engineers together at one end of the bar and the crews at the other. They tried to keep themselves in one party.

The time came when I had to leave all this. I signed on the old *St. Salacon*, one of Butts' 'S' boats–a white funnel with a black S on the side. It was a small bridge-aft-side vessel, with open bows, bound for the Faroes.

* * * * *

Steaming north from the Spurn Light Vessel, with the log line streamed and the watch set for steaming, the crew took turns at the wheel for one hour each. We drank a lot of tea, so we kept the kettle boiling at all times.

The net was overhauled and stoped during the passage up north. Passing a few ships coming home, we always blew 'Cock a Doodle Doo' on the whistle, entering in the log book the ship's name and the time we passed each other.

We had to pass through the Pentland Firth, twenty two miles of treacherous water even when there was no wind. Seven tides met somewhere in the Firth all at once, making the steering very awkward to keep on a set course. Sometimes we went sideways, the tide going faster than the ship. Many trawlers, even big boats, were lost in the Firth.

During fog you could hear many horns, blowing from different dangerous rocky points, the sounds all being listened to carefully to note where we were.

Steaming past Sinclair's Bay in the north east of Scotland, one of our engineers who had become friendly with me showed me Queen Victoria sat on her throne, in the form of rocks in the bay. While steaming towards Duncansby Head he told me to look in a westerly direction at the rocks and, as we steamed past, the rocks began to form the Queen sitting as if on her throne, just for a few seconds, and then it had gone. I wondered how many fishermen knew of this.

Many times afterwards I passed these rocks and showed someone else. Of course the weather had to be clear and calm.

Going through the Firth was a very beautiful sight to see. During a September evening, when things were very quiet, you could see through it for the twenty two miles, and see all the islands in the Orkneys and, on the mainland, some old castles. Even the remains of ships that had been driven ashore in the gales could be seen. One large vessel was shown to me through binoculars, miles away in a field. It had been washed ashore during a very bad storm, and had finished up in this field of potatoes.

Just now it was very calm with a few large gulls flying about, the mate saying: 'You always know when you are near the Firth, these big black gulls have white legs.' I thought he was joking. Many seagulls have red legs, or yellow. I remembered this later.

When we had passed through the Pentland firth that first time, we altered our course and steered north again, passing the Old Man of Hoy on the starboard side. Our engineer asked me to keep looking at this large rock as it would change into a man's face. I looked, and as we were passing it the large face came into place, reminding me of a Red Indian chief looking out to sea. I saw this many more times during my trips to the Faroes and Iceland.

We were now in the north Atlantic. Noticing a white line appear to starboard, I looked through the binoculars and saw the sight of my life: there were thousands of dolphins swimming from east to west. What a sight! There must have been a line of them a mile long by a quarter of a mile wide.

I also saw a few whales cleaning themselves by throwing themselves up into the air then coming down banging themselves on the water. A few sharks basking was a common sight, their large fins showing like small sailing boats.

At the end of one watch, seeing a very small white speck in the distance ahead, I thought it was a sailing ship. Reporting this to be the only object in sight, I went below off watch. Approximately eight hours later, coming up onto the bridge, I found the white speck that I had seen was Mount Snowy in Iceland. I had seen it from one hundred miles away.

* * * * *

During my watch below I read a little and the skipper would maybe tell us a bit of news that he had heard on his wireless. He had to keep the wireless off during the day time, the battery only lasting so many hours.

I remember the skipper saying he wanted a lead sounding during the following day. We dropped a larger lead than we had used in the North Sea and had to use the winch to heave it up from 200 fathoms or more. We carried on until he thought he was clear of the Monken Rocks that lay just below the surface of the sea at high tide and showed very little at low tide. They were a few miles to the south of Sudroy, the southerly part of the Faroe Islands.

I was told that the Faroes consisted of thirty-eight islands, eighteen of them were inhabited then. Keeping clear of the rocks we steamed on, the skipper saying it would not be long before we were going into the fiords to anchor in Vestermanshaven [Vestmanhavn]. We dropped anchor in the bay.

I remember seeing a very old Grimsby smack moored on the bankside, broken up and not seaworthy, in Vestermanshaven, about 1934 or '35. The name of this vessel was carved in the wood aft. It was the *Robert the Devil*, and was over 100 years old.

I believe it belonged to T. C. & F. Moss, or was out of that firm, because in later years in Tom Moss's office I recall seeing a picture of a racehorse and under the picture was the name

Robert the Devil.

I often wondered if there was any connection between the two names and if there was a small boy named Robert, who was a bit of a tartar or devil, and they named the ship and the race horse after him. Who knows?

When we anchored small ships' rowing boats came alongside. Some of the older fishermen who had been here before had brought soap and cigarette papers with them to barter for the woollen guernseys the Faroese people had made. I hadn't brought anything to barter with so I got a guernsey for two balls of twine I found in the forehold.

We had to scrub the fishroom out as we had filled it with coal in Grimsby which we needed to use for the five hundred odd mile trip. The trawl was ready to use but we were not allowed to put the otter doors over the side inside the fishing limit. Some skippers had been fined for this.

Sometimes fishing in the Faroes' waters, where the Gulf Stream runs, you have to lay-to during the daytime. The only thing you catch during daylight is jelly fish–or as we call them, sluthers. The trawl is full of them at certain times of the year. We laid-to during one nice day and I thought I would have a swim while waiting for daylight to go, and dived in, in eighty odd fathoms of very cold water. I was very glad to get back on board. I was gasping for my breath and I did not do that any more,

We hauled at night time and caught some beautiful fish. Faroe fish is very light coloured, haddocks, cod, plaice, dabs, all very light in colour, and plenty of food inside them too. They eat mussels, whelks, small herrings, and are rich in vitamins. Sometimes we left these grounds and fished on the Faroe Banks, about sixty miles north-west of the islands. The cod there were as big as men, and haddocks like cod. By the time I had gutted a few of these fish I believed it, my wrists were twice the thickness they had been a few days earlier.

The crew told me about the grundybos, a small whale which

came to the islands each year, and about the people of Thorshaven chasing them into the fiord and killing them. The whole population, from the fishermen to the baker, went in for the kill, taking whatever meat they wanted, burying it so that it would last through the winter months.

In those days food was very scarce in the Faroes, with not many vessels taking food supplies there. The people lived mainly on fish and mutton. They told me that, many years ago, Saint Patrick left sheep on the islands, and today nearly every one of these islands has sheep still living on it.

During very bad weather we brought the ship back to the fiords and anchored in calm waters, waiting for the wind to drop. So we kept a very good anchor watch, taking four hour watches: the mate and his deckhand, third hand and his deckhand, skipper and a trimmer deckie. Sometimes the wind changed and the anchor dragged. We knew this by taking a bearing with the compass on an object ashore. If the bearing altered we called the skipper who gave orders either to move ship or let out more anchor cable.

On Christmas Day we were anchored with it snowing and blowing hard. The cook was doing his best to cook the Christmas dinner in the galley aft. I remember it was my watch off and when the decky called dinner time I didn't go for my dinner. I was thinking of the people at home enjoying themselves, then I was so tired that I fell asleep.

After a couple of days we finally left the islands. I could see the rocks Gog and Magog in the distance, and another rock which looked like a submarine. The skipper told me it had been fired on during the 1914 war by a ship believing it to be a sub. Hence it was now called Submarine Rock on the charts.

Back again on the Faroe Bank fishing we were catching such nice large cod that we only got three fish to a ten stone box. When we gutted these fish the livers were taken out. We either boiled them in a small steam boiler that we had fixed in the old toilet astern of the ship, or we put them in tin drums

45.

that we carried on board, which held about forty gallons, fastened to the ship's rail along the quarter deck. We received about 12/- per man if it was oil, 5/- per drum if livers. Iceland ships carried more drums.

When the first liver boilers were installed the steam came through a pipe from the engine room. A small valve turned on the steam inside the liver house. We had no lights inside these liver houses at the time so, if we needed to look inside the boiler the light from a match would do. As long as the lid had been opened for some time it was O.K., but if the lid was opened and a match struck immediately the gases would explode. A friend of mine, told it was his turn to be liver man, struck a match, making the gases explode. Boiling oil spilled onto his face and he died within a few minutes. Later on all ships carried a warning sign, **NO NAKED LIGHTS TO BE USED.**

The livers taken from these large cod were like white mufflers. One of the crew raised a laugh by hanging one around his neck. Gutting on deck, the liver baskets soon filled up. Any of the crew, even the engineers, gave a hand to carry the baskets aft, for the liver man to boil or put into drums.

Sometimes something would happen and we would have to leave off gutting for a few minutes. If that did happen no sooner was your back turned, than the molleys (sea gulls) flew on board and they empty the liver baskets in seconds.

The skate we caught were very large. When they were gutted we had to lower them down the fishroom by the jilson. The large halibut was gutted by the mate, it being his privilage to do this job. The large halibut was named a geni, and to turn one over was a feat in itself. They weighed from ten to forty stones. Most of the large fish were lousy with sea lice which stuck to them. We rubbed them with ice and the lice would fall off before we put the fish away.

Whilst we were out fishing coal was being burned up and the engineers were getting niggly because they had to reach deep in the bunkers for coal. So the trimmer had to pull his ashes up and then go into the bunker to trim coal. By now it would be filled to the top of the bunker at the front part and down to nothing at the stokehold end. He trimmed two sides, maybe twenty tons of coal having to be moved before he came out of the storm door in the engine room with his carbide lamp. He then had a wash down in the engine room, after heating up a bucket full of water with a steam pipe.

This was now done daily until the engineer told the skpper we should have to stop fishing and go home, as we only had enough coal left to reach Grimsby.

So ended my first trip to the Faroes. Coming home, the weather was cold but fine; the watch was set and the log streamed abreast of Suderoy. We set course for the Pentland Firth, with the wind very light but northerly. Everyone turned in bar the engineer on watch, the mate and myself.

Steaming at night time with the full moon it seemed as bright as day, I went aft to the galley. The engineer was having a breather in the hoodway to the engine room. He said it was a nice night, and had I seen the man's face in the moon. I said that I hadn't. He told me to look hard and on the right side of the moon a man's face would appear, with a beard. I said yes, I could see it now. He replied that if I looked again I would see a lady's face on the oppposite side. After lying on deck and staring into the moon I saw a lady's face with long tresses on her hair. I've seen it many times since, on a full moon. Try it; but you must concentrate by staring into the moon.

He also showed me the Plough, the Pole Star and many others. We used to talk quite a lot and I asked him where he came from. He said he had been in Strangeways Jail, Manchester, for a murder but a nicer man I could not have met.

During the big coal strike, steam trawlers had to bunker in Belgium, the cheapest coal there being briquettes. These were made in great numbers in Belgium. Coal dust was mixed with tar, put in moulds and set to cool shaped much like large goose eggs. The ships' bunkers were filled with these briquettes which had to make steam for the ships. The engineers went into the stokehold like yo-yo's. No sooner was the furnace filled up, than the tar went up in one big flame, a fuelling did not last long and the furnace soon had to be filled up again.

Some of the vessels I sailed in still had their wing bunkers full of these briquettes which weren't used up intil we had a longer trip than usual, or perhaps held up by bad weather and had used all the coal in the main bunkers and sometimes the after fishroom, if a longer than usual trip–such as to the Faroes–had been planned.

During very bad weather we once called at the Vesterman Islands for water. We had run out of fresh water and needed some, both for the boilers and to drink. The people, I thought, were more Americanised than Icelandic.

We filled our tanks with water and I noticed that on the quayside there were piles and piles of fish heads. Whatever they did with them I did not know. But what amazed me were the big black rats running over them.

When we were steaming home and on watch during the night, the decks were alive with rats running all over. When we docked in Grimsby they were the first ashore. While we were putting the roopes on the bollards the rats jumped ashore onto the quay side and away.

Many ships I went fishing in had rats aboard. Being on watch during the night time,. towing the trawl, I have seen the rats take fish out of the baskets on deck, and take the plaice or other small fish in their mouths to the fo'c'sle and under the whaleback to eat it. Sometimes when in your bunk, and very tired, you could feel the rats tugging at your boot-stockings, taking the wool off for their nests.

The chief engineer of one ship had a rat in the engine room. He used to whistle it out during his watch and feed it, a big brown rat. I saw it once, crossing a pipe in the engine room.

48.

The second engineer got to know about this, and not liking rats about, he made a very thin snood with fuse wire. Eventually he caught this rat and killed it. When he came down to the dock for his pay after landing, they told him he had got the sack, for catching the chief's rat.

On another ship menaced by rats, we had a hose pipe raid on them, under all the boards in the chain locker. We finished up catching eleven. Several jumped overboard and the big gulls quickly swallowed them.

With rats and bugs and suchlike on these old ships, some had to be stoved out during the times the vessels had repair work done on their engines. Every item of clothing and bedding was taken off the ship and some chemicals were blown down the ship's bottom and sides, under the cabin floor boards, in bunks and in the chain locker, to drive out and kill the rats and bugs.

Today no ship should have any vermin aboard with the cleaning gear supplied nowadays. Then we were supplied with a small piece of soap, two boxes of matches, and a sweat rag each trip, per man. Toilet rolls none, they had not been invented then; we had to use newspaper or pieces of waste rag.

Coming home from the Faroes on one ship on which I was trimmer, we were running short of coal. After the main bunkers were emptied the engineers had to open the wings. These wings were the small, narrow spaces between the ship's sides and the boilers, maybe three feet wide from the stokehold to the engine room, around four or five tons of coal in each side. This ship had never used these wings since going to Belgium and filling up with briquettes. After being dried a long time they did not last very long, and I had to go in the back of the wings with a carbide lamp and shovel the briquettes into the stockhold for the engineer to put on the fire, to keep full steam up.

Rats made their home in these warm briquettes. We saw

many young rats in nests when digging these 'eggs' out coming home short of coal.

On one trip I was shovelling briquettes and rats out at the same time, the engineer killed many with his shovel. I cleared both wings of rats and briquettes before reaching the River Humber, and we just made it to the quayside, with no coal or steam left.

Coming home and seeing land on the port side was exciting. The Orkney Islands stood out clear, as did Torness where we turned into the notorious Pentland Firth, graveyard of hundreds of ships over the years. The tide, if it was with us, took us through to Duncansby Head very quickly. Passing the Isle of Stroma on the port side we turned into the North Sea, passing Sinclair's Bay, this time to starboard.

Remember, we had had the wireless for the first two weeks, but by now the batteries had run down, and we wanted to know the exact time. We steamed down the east coast of Scotland. Coming towards Peterhead we passed very close to land and the skipper took the time from the prison clock with his binoculars; at the same time Trinity House lookout would inform our office we were on our way home.

In later ships on which I sailed to the Faroes, we had a wireless telephone installed. The skipper could speak to other ships and report to Cullercoats radio station which, in turn, would pass messages to our homes at a cost which was taken from our liver or liver oil money.

We could see Whitby high land, and shortly after the Flamborough Head. Thirty-two miles to go, and then Spurn Light Vessel, we turned to starboard, passing the Chequer shoal buoy, Spurn lighthouse, the Bull Light Vessel and the two forts which have been named Bull Sand Fort and Haile Sand Fort for the past seventy years or so. We came to our anchorage again at the Burcomb Light Vessel.

We washed down in a bucket of water from the engine room, after cleaning down the fo'castle and wheelhouse, whilst the engineers had cleaned the engine room; the cook cleaning the cabin and skipper's berth. The net had been cleaned and rolled up like a large sausage, stretched from gallow to gallow and fastened with chains and strands of rope. The life lines we had put up whilst sailing home were stowed away for the next trip.

Coming into the dock, it was the same old story: I had been given the sack–a more experienced man was needed. Landing time was 4.00 a.m.

I came down to help land our catch with lumpers and crew having been asked to pull on the bell ropes–four ropes attached to a pulley wheel and four men pulling to a wheel. If the catch was bigger, more wheels were required. On big ships I have seen four or five wheels with twenty men pulling the baskets out of the hold onto landing boards. Ship by ship we landed, then steamed onto the quayside, putting the landing boards from the quay onto the gallows bar. The hatchway man swung the basket with its fish packed tightly inside, and the trimmer caught the basket and pushed it safely ashore where it was dealt with by the sorting out lumpers, weighed, and put on show for the merchants to buy.

As I previously said, the fish was looked after carefully when it was stored in the fish hold, and it was taken out as if it was still alive. All the fish had been properly gutted. Plaice was gutted with the left hand holding the fish, middle finger pressing on the gut, thumb holding the gill, and the sharp knife making a half moon cut under the gill, not damaging any of the flesh, so that when the merchants filleted the plaice they had two nice clean fillets. With cod, we made a nice clean cut in the belly, enough to take liver and gut out without damaging any flesh.

S.T. MacDuff

One vessel out of Grimsby, I remember, went to Greenland

just to fish for halibut and landed her catch near the swing bridge. When landing the lumpers dare not stick hooks into the flesh; each hook had to be put into the gill or mouth of the fish. I saw this ship sail out of Grimsby many times. She was the *McDuff*, and not much bigger than a seiner. She was used for line fishing. It used to fascinate me when I watched the lumpers land her catch of halibut and large cod. They were dragged on special coconut matting to the pontoon where they were on display for the buyers. If any were marked by the hooks the lumper responsible was given the sack.

This little ship was not much bigger than a seiner but she went to Greenland waters fishing.

I watched as the men coaled her in hundredweight bags, stacked forward in the bows, all around aft, and on the small galley top. I noticed that when she left harbour, the scuppers were under water.

After calling at Scrabsters for the coal bunkers to be refilled, she would set off for the Faroes (where sometimes salt herrings were bought for bait) or maybe for Iceland. More coal, water, and ice were taken aboard, then on to Greenland. Not much coal was used fishing as they moved about slowly when retrieving lines.

The drill was the same coming home. They were saving the halibut for most of the trip. Any large cod were put below, if there was any room for them, only on the last day of fishing.

Fog was a hazard. While steaming, we had to use the whistle quite a lot. It was mounted fore-side of the funnel and blown every three minutes or so. If ships were passing, we blew until all was clear.

I remember one trip, bound for the Faroes. We left Grimsby docks in thick fog, only just able to see the inside of the lock pits. We made a trip to the Faroes and back again without seeing anything at all until coming into dock again. Using the hand lead and whistle, we listened to different light houses and light vessels blowing their horns. You had to be very near the light vessels to see their flashing lights.

On one trip, when we were coming up the Humber, we stopped the engines, to listen for the Bull Light Vessel's signal, when I heard voices speaking. I shouted to the men I could hear, and they asked me if I was swimming. I told them I was on a trawler's bow, and asked where we were. The two men were fishing off the fort.

We steamed easterly for a while before setting course for the Burcombe Light Vessel. Eventually coming to the fishdocks, we found ourselves inside the Royal Dock Basin. Fog signals seemed to be blowing everywhere.

Another time, on one of Butts' ships going to the Faroes, (again in thick fog), it was thought to be too dangerous to go through the Pentland Firth during foggy weather. So the skipper ordered the mate to drop anchor as we were in Sinclair's Bay in the northeast of Scotland. After several anchor watches, daylight appeared. The skipper asked me if the fog had cleared. I told him that I could see land, and he asked: 'How does the land bear?'

I said, 'Westerly'. He came into the wheelhouse and could not believe his eyes. We had drifted during the night right through the Pentland Firth, twenty miles or so, in thick fog, and could now see the Old Man of Hoy.

On another trip home from the Faroe Islands in thick fog, I was on watch; we were steaming southerly. I pulled the whistle rope inside the wheelhouse to make one long blast, intending to do this every three minutes. The skipper gave me the order to stop blowing the whistle because the course we were sailing on meant that we should not see another ship for two hundred miles.

During the following hour or so, the engineer on watch, a man called Tupplin–a one time boxer known as the Fighting Fisherman– came up to the bridge to move the ventilators off the wind. As we stood talking I saw a white wave appear on the port side. In a second I saw a ship pass, not many feet from us, in the thick fog. The name of the ship was the *Perhelion*, one of Letton's, bound for Greenland.

We did not stop blowing the whistle after that.

I wonder how many ships were lost for not using the whistle, and with no wirelesses to use to call for help.

During the voyages to and from the Faroes, we encountered very bad weather–storms, very severe gales, snow storms, and frost. On very frosty nights it seemed the frost killed the wind, and we could see the Aurora Borealis hundreds of miles away, the Northern Lights flashing off the ice in all colours of the rainbow. It is a sight that is out of this world!

The sea, when angry, was a menace. Steering the ship was not easy, the wheel knocking you over when the ship rolled, and with the waves coming inboard and washing any loose gear overboard. On one trip he liver jars or barrels which had been lashed to the ship's side disappeared. The wind howled through the rigging and the halyards were lashed on the foremast. The small lifeboat that we had on the after deck lost its mounting and lay on its side with a large hole in it.

The skipper came up from below and asked if we had seen any flashing lights and, if not, to stop engines and lay until daylight. He went below again. The third hand, whose watch I was in at the time, was named Bye. He came from a fishing family and knew his job. He said to call the trimmer and tell him to pull the ashes up whilst we were laid.

Dawn was just breaking; the waves on the starboard side were the size of the ice house in Victor Street, one after the other. One minute we were on top of a mountain, next thing we were in a valley. 'I hope that lot does not break over us,' I said to myself.

The trimmer pulling the ashes up had just emptied the bucket on deck. Next time I looked at him he was holding the bucket ropes, hanging perpendicular. I thought he was going overboard, but he hung on, swearing and cursing at the weather.

At daylight the cook came out, swearing about the galley fire being out, and the pots and pans being all over the floor. 'I'll keep clear of him today,' I thought.

The third hand said the anchor had come adrift forward and he was going to lash it down again; would I keep my eye on the waves, and if there were any breaks, to warn him by shouting 'Water!' He made the anchor fast again and started to put a lashing here and there on the trawl. He had come over to the lee side of the ship when one wave broke over the midships and tons of water poured over the side, catching him. I thought he had gone over the side.

When the water subsided and the ship came up again he was hanging onto the barrel of the winch, wringing wet through. He went below, put on a dry set of clothes and came on the bridge, rang the telegraph for full speed ahead and did not say another word all the watch.

After leaving the Faroes, the wind being westerly and, at times, gale force, the waves were twenty to thirty feet high, maybe more at times, and the trawler I was on during that trip was not much larger than a seiner going to sea today. The ship was made of iron, not wood. It was steam driven and could make a good 11 knots through the water, by the ship's log.

The waves coming up on the starboard side made huge walls of water, the ship was shuddering with the helmsman pulling the wheel to starboard to meet the rising swell–then down she went again into a large trough. The little stormy petrels, small sea birds with webbed feet and no bigger than a starling, were diving and weaving in and out from trough to trough, keeping out of the wind, feeding on fragments of plankton floating on the water. Fisherman say they are becoming extinct now; not many nests are seen on Rockall or Sule Skerry and the small rocky islands where they breed. If you see any of these birds, it's a bad weather sign, you don't need a barometer to tell you.

A few hours later we were through the Pentland Firth and into calm water heading south and home.

CHAPTER 5

SCRAMBLING THE NET ABOARD

PULLING THE NET ABOARD IN BAD WEATHER was no easy task in these side winders.

Not catching a lot of fish, the coal being burnt up, food running low, morale low, and the weather getting worse by the hour, with no time to dodge or go into harbour for shelter. The skipper decides to put the gear down and fish, saying he will give us a chance to get the fish gutted and put below before shooting the gear away again and have a couple or three days more fishing to try and get a trip together.

It is now blowing hell's bells and we are towing the gear: the cook is having a ball trying to cook the meals and the engineers, trying to shovel coal into the furnaces, are more likely to put coal in the bunkers again. The ship is lighter now, so she's rolling and pitching more, you have a job to keep your feet whatever you may be doing.

* * * * * *

'Haulo, Haulo,' the watch shouts down the hatchway. Boots and oilskins are hurriedly found. First out, best dressed, they told me. Out of the hatchway and onto the deck. You hear the skipper shout: 'Knock out, knock out,' and whoever is on watch pulls the pin out of the towing block, giving it a bash with the big hammer and away. The two warps part, one being heaved forward and one aft, through their respective rollers.

The mate and deckhand on the winch watch for short marks coming up on the warps. Seeing those two short marks is of great importance. You have to slow the speed on the winch until the skipper has the ship with the wind on the starboard side or, if using the portside trawl, to port.

Ship stopped: doors up, Dan Lenos up: quarter ropes on winch drums bobbing aboard. Headline grabbed by six or seven pairs of hands and: 'Heave ho, heave ho,' the mate yells at the top of his voice; we are all pulling the net in.

'When she rolls,' he'll shout, the waves now twenty feet high, more net going back than inboard.

'When she rolls,' it's the skipper shouting now, 'get the bloody thing aboard.'

A new wave now coming breaks. Everyone shouts: 'Water!' meaning let go of everything and jump onto the life bar under the bridge or onto the engine room casing out of reach of the water that has come aboard.

Many trawler men have been pulled overboard because they were wearing wedding rings. Some have lost fingers, their rings catching in the net whilst it was being washed back again during bad weather.

The ship would shudder and settle down a bit. 'Come on, get that bloody headline and be a bit smarter this time, Mr. Mate.'

And so it would go on until the same old story:–no food, no coal–meant that we'd have to go home, fish or no fish.

Fish below, hatches battened down. Life lines rigged up, deck boards made fast, liver jars chained down, the trawl neatly stowed on the starboard side and lashed down tightly. The ashes pulled up and dumped on deck, the watch set, log streamed, and the telegraph rung 'Ahead'; and we'd be steaming home once more in a northerly gale.

THE TRIMMER ON BOARD STEAM TRAWLERS

It is my belief that the trimmer's work on any steam trawler was the hardest work anyone did for a living. You had to be eighteen years of age to be a trimmer, a deckhand could be younger. On leaving–and on entering–the dock his job was to stand aft on the vessel and make sure that the vessel did not damage itself on the lock sides, as the tide sometimes swings the stern on to the stone lockpit sides. Putting the fender in between ship and shore saves a lot of damage being done.

His next job, going down the river, was to fill the cabin lockers with coal so that the cabin fire could be kept alight all through the trip. The paraffin navigation lights on the wheelhouse had to be cleaned and trimmed, and new wick and paraffin provided ready to light before dark. The masthead lights, the fishing lights, and the stern lights, had all to be cleaned before dark each day by the trimmer. The mending needles, too, had to be filled with tarry twine in case the net should need mending.

But the most important job he had to do was trim the coal in the bunkers for the boiler fires, trimming maybe ten tons a day in all weathers: he would be thrown about in the bunkers with large pieces of coal falling on top of him. The coal heaps, trimmed once, may have had to be thrown back again. His only light would be a small carbide lamp that he had put up: sometimes this would be knocked and put out, making the trimmer climb out of the small hole he had to go through and relight the lamp.

Clearing the ashes from the furnace was the trimmer's job. He had to pull up in buckets and empty them over the ship's side into the sea. Not all this work was without danger. The ashes had to come up out of the stokehold after each engineer's watch, maybe two fires being cleaned, making a twenty bucket pull. Sometimes, if the engineer damped the ashes too much, the buckets became very heavy and it was hard work getting them up on deck through the ventilator by a rope and pulley.

During gales of wind, most trimmers tied a rope round their body in case a wave knocked them overboard.

I remember pulling the ashes up, coming home from the Faroes during a very bad night. The wind was howling through the rigging, and waves were fifty to sixty feet high: it was very frightening. A wave hit the starboard side as I was pulling some ashes up. The small lifeboat we had aft went overboard, the top of the mainmast went too. I was holding the ash poles like grim death, my legs over the side of the port rail, until the ship came back onto an even keel again and I could continue with my job.

Very nearly all the wire heaving was the trimmer's job.

Coming into the river the trimmer had to scrub the cabin and one of the worst aspects of the job was being always at the beck and call of the rest of the crew–being the least in rank.

During fishing operations he had to heave the two warps together, with the messenger wire, then the third hand would block the two wires together aft.

Later, after the trawl was fishing again, he would help to gut the catch. Just before the fish was ready to be washed he would give a knock on the ship's casing with a ring bolt which was attached. This knocking gave the signal for the enginer on watch to start the donkey pump for the hosepipe on deck to wash the fish. Then he would go down to the fish room to chop ice on which the fish would be laid or covered with. If you shelved your fish you laid it on the top of the ice, if you bulked the fish you covered it all round with ice. This ice could be very hard at times, like glass, making the trimmer sweat, trying to break it up.

So I believed the trimmer's job required tough hard working men, sometimes having no sleep for days on end. And all this for £1 18s. 6p per week.

THE FAROES

Faroe Dan was skipper of the Grimsby trawler *Susarion* (which was lost in 1944). I sailed with him as trimmer before the war, in W.W. Butts' firm.

He fished the islands and brought his cod into Grimsby. His family lived on the Faroe Islands. I remember when we steamed into Vestermanshaven to repair our tanks ready for fishing. He pointed out many features and rocks to me, some that I was seeing for the first time such as Gog and Magog, the Submarine

Rock, Fuglo, the Monks' Rocks, which could be seen on leaving the islands coming south, and the last small island, Sudero. As we passed this island the skipper blew the whistle on the funnel. If the people on the lighthouse could not hear us they could see the steam coming out of the whistle, and stood waving a white cloth to us. The skipper told us that it was his sister who looked after the lighthouse.

TUNNY FISHING

Fishing in the trawlers in the North Sea in late summer, in very calm water, it surprised me to see thousands of herrings swim past on either side of the ship. The oil from the fish floated to the top of the water when the herring had dived deeper after hearing the sound of our propellor swishing round.

The herring must be the most chased fish in the sea. Every nation is fishing for them and almost every fish in the sea eats them, from the smallest to the fully grown. They swim very fast, I counted sixteen fins on a herring. The cod thrive on them, turbots eat them and dozens of other fish hunt for them.

One fish that I recall is the tunny fish, one of the fastest swimming fish in the sea. During the summer months before the war, the weather seemed to be a lot hotter, and the North Sea had many tunny fish hunting the herring: and hunting the tunny were the millionaires with their large yachts and many rods and lines. During the day, their small boats were lowered and away the anglers went, fishing, many calling at the trawlers for bait, which was quickly given in exchange for a bottle of spirits and a box of cigars or cigarettes.

The Danes had their own way of catching the tunny. They used a twenty foot pole with hook and line baited with one whole herring, which was tied to the hook with a piece of string cotton and dangled overboard. The strong line carrying the baited hook was coiled on deck in one hundred fathom lengths, and a large bladder was hung over the ship's rail tied to the line.

60.

After the tunny took the baited hook, the cotton broke off the pole, and as the fish taking the herring swam away at sixty to seventy miles per hour coils of rope disappeared off the deck with the bladders being towed by the tunny fish. After the fish has tired itself it is hauled back to the ship by a small winch.

I saw ten tunny caught in this fashion one day by a Danish vessel fishing alongside us.

SHARKS

There is a small variety of shark that comes for herring too. They also are caught by the Danish boats and taken back to Denmark.

The method of catching these is by a floating fishing line. A Dan buoy is laid with a line attached, one float–a piece of cork painted white–one baited hook, six feet of snood, then another float and hook, until about two to three miles of baited hooks and corks are floating on top of the water, then lastly the other Dan buoy.

After about four hours fishing (day or night) the sharks are taken off the hooks, which are rebaited again and again for two week periods–then home for a few days before returning and fishing again.

During my life fishing in trawlers we caught a few sharks in the North Sea and we were asked by the firms that I sailed with to bring them home and land them. They said that we would get a good price for them. The biggest one that we sold was to Mudds, which was a large shop in London; there the shark was hung up for show. We got five shillings for it.

On another ship, we caught a large shark and we left it on deck. During the day I wondered if it had died or if it was just waiting for someone to have a bite at. I did not like the look of it so kept my distance from it when moving about the deck.

The chief engineer, Ben Jermany, came on deck for a bit of fresh air and gave the shark a tap on the nose with a piece of wood we had picked up in the net. The shark turned round snapping its jaws inches from Ben's legs. He went pale and went below. I never saw him on deck again that trip.

THE TRAWLERS

The old steam trawlers had many faults. During fishing operations they frequently had to be repaired whilst at sea; winches breaking down, warps parting, and the longest repair (and I believe the worst to happen) was tubes bursting inside the boilers, putting the furnace fires out. These tubes went through the boilers and the fire was beneath the tube or tubes. It depended on how many tubes burst and had to be repaired or blanked off as to how long the repair took, and how long the boilers were out of action. But however many tubes burst it meant that someone had to go into the furnace to do this repair work.

First the steam has to be let off and then the furnace allowed to cool down. The law stated that a period should be allowed for cooling down and it should be twenty-four hours, before anyone was allowed to enter the boiler: but the law in those days was the skipper. He was up and down the engine room ladder after about four hours saying to the chief that he was losing fishing time and would like the repair work done; the engineer saying that it was too hot to go into the furnace and they both kept arguing.

I remember Old Ben Jermany, a chief engineer of steam trawlers, was one of the best engine men out of Grimsby. He made many trips to sea with me in various ships, a good old grafter if there ever was one.

If the fishing stopped because of a defect in the engine room, or if the boiler tubes stared to leak, putting the coal fires out, he would confer with the skipper and ask him to lay to until the damage had been repaired, instead of coming home with no fish. He would try his hardest to fish again.

One day whilst fishing in one of our old tubs, the tubes burst. We had to haul the trawl, then lay to until Old Ben had a look to see if he could repair them.

Calling his mate to go with him, into the stokehold he told the second engineer to pull the fires and clear the furnace of any ashes. This being done and all the ashes and coal damped down, the trimmer pulled all this up, bucket by bucket, and emptied the lot over the lee side rail into the sea. The stokehold and furnace now cleared, Old Ben lit a carbide lamp and had a look into the furnace, trying to find which tubes were leaking.

The furnace should have at least twenty four hours cooling down before anyone entered the firedoors, where there was only just enough room to squeeze through.

The fire bars were still hot, so Ben asked me if we could put pound boards inside the furnace for him to crawl on. The tubes were at the back of the furnace and six hours had gone now and we were all getting bitchy with each other waiting for Ben to start the job.

He said that if we gave him a hand to get him into the furnace he would try to repair the tubes. He told us it was very hot inside with very little air, and smelt like sulphur. He put some roe bags round his hands and we lifted him up and pushed him inside, head first, then his shoulders. His feet were just sticking out of the fire doors when he shouted for us to pull him out as he had caught fire inside. We had a long hard pull to get him out of such a small hole. We found it was the boards which were alight inside. He was frothing at the mouth, but O.K.

We had to wait many more hours before the furnace had cooled enough. We set the watch and had some sleep while waiting. The second engineer helped Ben to repair the tubes, taking it in turns.

Then the fires were lit again, and it was top steam. Eventually we fished again and caught a trip to come home with and land–thanks to Old Ben.

Whilst talking to Old Ben in the engine room I saw a few wooden pegs in the ship's side and asked him what they were. He hit the ship's side with the small head of a hammer and knocked a hole in the plate, at the same time taking a piece of wood from a small cupboard. He put this into the hole and belted it with the hammer, stopping the flow of water coming in. He said next time the ship had a refit he would have another plate put in.

Many times during bad weather fishing, or when it was blowing hard, the winch on deck would require new packing in the pistons, steam coming out of the winch ends was stopping the trawl coming up. The engineers had to come on deck out of the warm into the freezing cold to do these repairs, sometimes taking a few hours to complete them.

Many engineers lost fingers repairing engines whilst a ship was stopped, because of the waves breaking onto the propellor and turning the engines when the engineer was working between the rods and prop-shaft. Trawling was a dangerous job both on deck and below.

I would often look down at the engine room skylight from the lee side of the deck and see the engineer oiling the piston plates as the engine was turning at full speed. Up and down his oil can would move, seeming with the speed of light, not touching any part of the piston rods as they turned the propellor shaft. Sometimes I would hear him saying: 'Now what's the matter with you, Mary?' or some other name that he had for various parts of the engine. He would call it by name and say: 'I'm coming to oil that squeaky noise,' and if the second engineer came on watch he would tell him about the squeak and to keep his ears open in case it happened again and got worse.

On the deck casing there was a hole cut out, with a lid attached, so that the engineer could turn a valve off and on. On top of the boilers, under the lid, was an iron grid; in fine weather this was kept open for ventilation, then shut down during gales. There was another grid behind the funnel from where it was possible to look down and see the engineers firing the furnace, the heat from the fires burning your face at times, especially when the engineer was pulling a fire, which he had to do to keep the fire clean before the ashes were damped down before they were dumped overboard.

After fishing watches, if we had caught some nice large cod, I would put some cod livers in a large tobacco or cigarette tin and, with a piece of wire for a handle, hang it down the fiddly grid near the funnel. After a few days had passed, on the way home, I would syphon the oil from the tin through blotting paper that I had taken with me, bottling the pure cod liver oil and taking it home for my family who liked to drink it for health reasons.

I remember walking into the ship's husband's office in Fishdock Road–E. Bacon's firm–and being asked to go as fireman in one of their ships to Faroe. I said that I had not fired a ship before, and he said: 'Everyone has to start the first time,' so I signed on as fireman-decky. This meant that I had to fire the ship whilst steaming to the fishing grounds, then work on deck and take my watch whilst fishing. Coming home I had to go below again and fire the ship.

The ship being coaled, watered, iced, and stored, we left Grimsby. The second engineer told me that I would be in his watch. Leaving the Humber and steaming northerly I had to take my first watch.

The weather was not too good and the ship did a bit of rolling. The fishroom was full of coal, and about fifteen more tons were in the tunnel leading to the after fishroom. The drill was that, after the coal had been used up in the tunnel, we started to use coal from the fishroom, starting down the middle and keeping the coal level on both sides as it was burnt up.

During a watch you fired the ship then trimmed the coal, the next watch doing the same, leaving each watch an hour's rest before starting trimming again. The nearer we got to the Faroes, the further we had to shovel the coal, sometimes taking three throws with the shovel to the end of the tunnel from where we first started. At the journey's end, the coal having been burnt up from the tunnel and fishroom, we'd leave a small amount of coal in the tunnel and seal the outer end with a thick iron door which was turned by wheel to close it very tight. This kept warm air from going into the fishroom which was then washed out by the crew and made ready for fish to be iced and stowed.

As it was my first trip on the fires I had to learn the hard way. The second engineer, being no friend of mine, did his job and expected me to do mine. I had to rake the fire with a large iron rod about ten feet long, I could hardly lift it. It rested on a small crossbar under the fire and I had to prick the crust of the fire to let the ashes fall into the pit. This was done nearly every fifteen minutes before coal was put on the three furnaces which we had on this ship. Raking the fire, putting the coal on, trimming coal, filling the ash buckets up for the trimmers to pull up and throw overboard, filling the tunnel end with coal for the following watch, rolling about, being sea-sick. I was glad to get on deck, gutting and washing fish, and in the fresh air.

After the fishing finished and it was time to start for home, I had to take my watch again. This time the coal was in the main bunkers, which made it a lot easier to work. The engineer gave me a hand to fire the ship. Whilst inside the bunkers, shovelling the coal from forward to aft, the only light I had was a carbide lamp the engineer had lent me because the bunkers were very dark and damp. I could see leaking rivets everywhere I looked and I got wet through if I rolled onto the ship's side. The only entrance to the bunkers was the storm door, a small square hole cut out near the deckhead just big enough to get one leg over at a time.

Coming home from Faroe in a trawler, a very great fishing friend of mine, still living in Grimsby, lost one eye at sea. When he was firing the ship, a hot cinder, blowing out of the furnace while he was in the stockhold, went into his eye and burnt it.

He put a handkerchief round his eye and carried on working until the vessel reached Grimsby. He found that he had lost that eye.

I remember two miners going to sea as trimmers to find out what it was like. They went on one trip, and then they were back down the mines.

And that was what I thought of firing when I got back to Grimsby, a one-trip fireman.

CHAPTER 6

THE WEATHER AGAIN

WRITING THESE STORIES ABOUT FISHING is a constant reminder about weather. Today, on the telly, you see a map in the morning and a young girl and lad tell you what is likely to happen during the day. At night time, you have the weather experts giving you their version of what's likely to happen.

During my fishing days everything happened so quickly it would take us by surprise, like the storms we had whilst fishing in the North Sea. You might say: 'North Sea–but it's like a park pond!' It's roughly two hundred miles wide and approximately one thousand miles long and, believe me, it can get rough.

I remember being on board the *S.T. St. Cedric,* T.C. & F. Moss firm, Fishdock Road. The skipper was Jimmy McCan from Cleethorpes, and I was a trimmer on the ship.

The doors and bobbins were laying over the starboard side; I was holding the net whilst the skipper and mate were mending it. Looking over the port side, on the horizon approximately thirteen miles away, I saw a white cloud and it seemed to me it was on the water coming towards us. There were a few ships in the vicinity of us at the time. I asked the skipper what he thought it might be.

Dropping the net and needle he was holding, he told the mate to get the gear aboard quickly and to batten down the fishroom and warn the engine room to batten down, as he thought we might have some very strong wind coming from the south east, a very unusual wind.

We battened down and began to dodge the ship into the Silver Pits where the water deepened to forty fathoms, and out of the swell that had begun to form. Other ships were not as lucky as we were; with the watch on the bridge and the crew below, sleeping, they had a rough time. Some of them were caught napping, leaving hatches open so that water poured into the fishrooms. A few coasters got into trouble, one coal carrier going down north of the river.

We lay to for ten days before we could fish again. The wind blew so hard that the sea became flat, like white foam. We had to put into Lowestoft, out of the weather.

Being very foggy one night, we drove onto the Haighbrough Sands, a sandbank which was so dangerous that many vessels have been lost on it. The wind started to blow from the east, the ship banging on the bottom, and the green coloured water was breaking over us. It was a very frightening position to be in.

Putting the rocket apparatus on the bridge verandah we sent the rockets towards Cromer. Very shortly we saw the answering rocket, to let us know the lifeboat was on its way.

Captain Blogg, double Lifeboat V.C., was in command and he knew where we had struck the bank. He stood by until daylight, when the wind dropping and the tide rose, then showed us the way to steam ourselves off. He escorted us into Lowestoft where the ship was examined for damage and repaired to let us get home. No-one was injured or lost.

Fishing on our own, in the old steam trawlers, miles from anywhere, we could see the horizon all around. Sometimes, on the bridge, looking around, we would see a mast moving in the distance. It looked very queer to see a large cargo or passenger ship passing, without seeing anything of the ship itself. The world being round, about thirteen miles and the horizon is all that there was to see, unless something was higher, and that mast I used to see at times must have been fourteen miles away, on a shipping lane.

We also used to see the smoke from other passing vessels.. Coal fired ships made a lot of smoke and that could be seen for miles without actually seeing anything of the vessels themselves. When spotting other trawlers on the horizon, the crew would try to guess the name of the ship. I was very good at naming ships by their outline from miles away. There was always something different from one another you could remember about them.

The old steam trawler, *Cedric*, was the first ship I was to sail in that had a dynamo. What a relief, no pulling lights up the mast, no port and starboard lights to trim and hang out on the sides of the wheelhouse, no stern light to hang up and no deck lights to light and look after. It seemed like a new era. I heard the gaffer, Tom Moss. tell the engineer the dynamo had cost a lot of money and he had to take care of it.

The *Cedric* was out of T.C. & F. Moss's office in Fishdock Road and belonged to the United Fishing Company, as was the steam trawler *Gurth*, and another ship which I cannot remember ever seeing was the *Ivanhoe*. These small ships sailed to Iceland in their young days.

I had a few more trips in the Noth Sea, fishing round the Shetland Isles. At the Island of Foula we had a large catch which turned out to be rat fish. I had not seen any of these before. A long thin tail they had, and when held up, resembled a rat's outline. We gutted the large ones, taking the liver out, and then dumping the lot overboard.

Then the Faroes again, and I thought I would see Mr. Rouse, the ship's runner for W. Butts' firm. I had been to the Faroes in the old *Salacon* and *Olympia* in his firm, but I wanted to go fishing to the White Sea on the Russian coast, for a change. It was now 1937.

I had plenty of experience and could now do almost anything that a decky might be asked to do. The time had come to try the big ships.

It was winter time, and I had stored my sea bag in Dobby's shop on the North Wall. I bought a new oil frock for 10/-, one pair of cotton gutting gloves (1/-), one sou'wester (2/-), one pair of mittens (2/6), one new donkey's breakfast, and my straw

70.

bed, (5/-); tying them up in a bundle and putting a label on them, I paid (1/-) for the store man to look after them for me. Meanwhile, a dozen fishermen were looking for their fishing gear amongst the hundreds of bundles left in the store room. My knife (1/-) went into my pocket. I had spent most of one week's wages–£1.18s. 6d. (one pound eighteen shillings and sixpence).

I signed on the steam trawler *Edwardian*, skippered by Parson John. The crew told me he had come from Ireland as a deckhand and had studied navigation etc. while at sea, reading nautical books in his spare time, and had earned his skipper's ticket very quickly He was very strict, did not swear, but he did and said things far worse. What he said was law. His crew did not leave, he only sacked the shirker, and the men who did leave were ill, or had personal reasons for leaving.

The Board of Trade rules allowed only twelve men in these ships; later on there were twenty or more. We had one skipper, one mate, one third hand, one cook, two engineers, two firemen, two deckhands, two trimmers. We also had one spare hand who went as wireless operator and boiled livers if there were no wireless duties. He kept up with the latest news and football results which he heard from Wick radio on Saturday at midnight. He tapped private telegrams to our homes for us through Cullercoats radio or Humber radio, which at that time was in Waltham near Grimsby. Further away, he could only morse to Wick radio or pass a message to be picked up by another ship which was nearer to land to be transferred for him.

Leaving Grimsby Docks on the early morning tide, we rigged the lifelines up above the port and starboard rails to stop anyone going over the side whilst going from forward to aft. During darkness we had no deck lights on, only the white mainmast steaming light and the port and starboard red and green lights, the stern light being behind the small lifeboat on the chocks astern. Each one of us had to grab a lifeline from forward hoodway to the winch, one of those that we had rigged up to help us in bad weather.

Steaming into a gale is very nasty so you try to be careful and take all sensible precautions. Everything that could move is fastened down, hatches and bunker lids greased and tightened down, the net has been hove tight on the starboard side and, like a giant sausage, neatly chained and roped to the ship's side.

The ship was not new and, unlike the new vessels being built, was only half the size of many deep sea trawlers and not as fast. But she was a good sea ship. The mate and skipper were on the bridge, sorting the watch out, whilst the third hand streamed the log: passing Spurn Light Vessel the clock was set to zero. Most of the crew were in the fo'c'sle forward making their beds up, getting their sea clothes on, and stowing their shore clothes away until required again.

A shout cane from the bridge asking the crew to muster there for their bond. Cigarettes, tobacco, tins of John West salmon (large tins, two for 2/6d), three tablets of Lux soap, perfumed, 1/- in a box. Chocolates of different varieties were asked for, and tins of sweets. The skipper did not allow any liquour to be drunk whilst steaming.

The watch was set after each man had got his bond. Three miles outside the dock and we were allowed to open the bond which had been sealed by the Customs Officer after it had come aboard from the bonded stores on the docks.

The crew were, by now, settling down, telling their stories of what they had been up to whilst in dock, who they had seen during their pub crawls and telling one another the names of ships their pals had joined. They had just missed them by a tide or a day and, with a bit of luck, would see them next time in dock. The women they had loved was a story in itself, if you believed half of it.

The mate took the first watch with a deckhand named Joey, so I had to be in the third hand's' watch, the senior deckhand taking a watch with the trimmer. The skipper was on hand if needed.

So off we went, very cold, with the wind blowing from astern and getting rougher by the hour. Steaming towards the Norwegian coast the seas became very choppy and several times large waves swept over the stern. The ship was shuddering as its arse lifted up and the propellor came up out of the water making a dreadful row. The crew in the fo'c'sle shut the halfdoor in the hoodways to stop the water going down. Whilst trying to get some shut-eye, one of the crew was thrown out of his bunk by a heavy lurch.

Entering the west fiords the ship was like a matchstick in a bucket of water. We put larger pound boards inside our bunks to keep us in.

On entering the fiords and getting into calmer waters I went up on deck to see the land and was surprised to see we had lost the small lifeboat from aft, during the night.

I have never seen a more wonderful sight than when I stayed up during my watch off. There were fir trees in their millions on the mountain sides, some with snow on them, and small wooden houses dotted here and there in all colours of the rainbow.

Our first call was Lodigen, a small pilot station on this island, where we picked up our first pilot to take us to Tromsö –the capital of The North, so they said. I was surprised to learn that we had another lifeboat waiting for us to put aboard, as the firm had left it at Tromsö so that if any of the firm's ships lost one it could be replaced. It was a regular occurence, they told me.

Mooring up at the ice terminal, the skipper disappeared with his friends and left the crew to prepare the ship for fishing, telling the mate to be ready in twenty-four hours. We had to scrub out the fishroom which had had coal in it for the long steam, and the Norwegian icemen filled the pounds with ice which had been brought from the mountains in rush covered barges in blocks and crushed before coming aboard. Food was very scarce in Norway at that time and, being on the Artic Circle, fish was the order of the day. The young lads and lassies all seemed to be on the quay-side fishing. As I watched, they were pulling fish up every minute; no bait, just shaking the hook about and a small coley would be caught and landed. After about half a dozen were caught the youngsters put a bit of twine through the gills and took them home.

were pulling fish up every minute; no bait, just shaking the hook about and a smmeal at tea time, the cook turned in, leaving the washing up for the watch. Being my turn on watch and my first night in Tromsö, I was talking to the young wireless operator when one of the Norwegians asked, in his own language, if he could do the washing up and clean the cabin table. The wireless operator said it was usual for the Norwegians to wash up as they would get a free meal for doing the job. When we offered the chap a meal he started to cry, tears streaming down his face. He told the wireless operator that his family had no food in the house and could he take home the food he was offered because he had three children.

The wireless operator, hearing the Norwegian's story, was very touched by it. The cook had baked six large loaves during the afternoon and, emptying a potato sack, the wireless operator put flour, loaves of bread, and several more items in it, and told the chap to hop it home, before the cook found out. What happened when the cook got up in the morning and found his bread locker empty is best left unsaid!

Tromsö is a large island in the north-west fiords above the Arctic Circle. When we moored the ship alongside the jetty the skipper pulled the cord in the wheelhouse and sounded the steam whistle which was on the foreside and top of the funnel. It made a very loud noise and, in the fiord, could be heard many miles away. Blowing the whistle was the signal that ice was required. It amused me to see about twenty men on ice bikes making their way downhill to the ship. They sat on a wooden seat and, instead of wheels, they had skis on them and came very fast. The first ones to the ship got the job of ice trimming.

The firemen refilled the fresh water tanks, the third hand put false bellies on the cod ends (these were old nets, or sometimes cow hides, used to protect the nets which were often damaged when they were trawled–dragged–over rocks and debris on the seabed), and I helped by going on top of the galley where we kept two wooden barrels filled with cowhides which were fastened on the outside of the cod ends. Getting two large pieces, I cut about eight holes in the tops of the cowhides and the third hand fastened them on. After the net had been overhauled, it was stowed away again for the long journey north.

I met quite a few Norwegians and gave them cigarette papers, of which it seemed they could not get enough. I found out that the ciagarette papers they did get had no sticky side on them. Oranges and apples were a godsend to them, soap and chocolates a luxury. Making friends, two Norwegian girls asked the other deckhand and me if we would like to go with them for a row. Going into the boat and down the fiords with them we saw a few whalers which were very smart looking vessels with the harpoon gun on the bow. The girls told us that they caught quite a lot of small whales in the fiords.

We saw a small steam tug towing about a dozen barges full of ice, taking it to the jetty to be broken up by the fishermen.

This being my first trip to the Arctic North, it was very exciting. Then the whistle blew from the *Edwardian*, letting us know that the skipper had come on board and wanted to cast off. We could not row the boat fast enough to get to the ship, so we let the two girls row us back. When we cast off, the small crowd gave us a wave off.

It was very cold and the small coal fire we had in the fo'c'sle was red hot. We had cleaned the stack whilst in Tromsö by putting an iron shackle down from the top and pulling it out of the fire with a large piece of bagging following to clean the hole all the way through. We had filled all the lockers with coal, so that we could dry out our cold and wet gear. In the new ships then being built proper drying rooms were included.

Steaming again, I took my turn on the wheel, the Norwegian pilot still giving orders to which points of the compass he wanted me to steam.

The fiords were a thousand miles long from the North Cape to Copperness, a passage that I sailed through during one trip coming home, the weather being too bad to steam outside the coast. The sights we saw were far too many to write about them all. We were steaming along with rocks all around one minute and open sea the next: seeing two posts sticking out of the water with no land in sight, and being told to steer between those two posts or we would run aground sounds silly but that is what it was like. The anchor was always at the ready to drop should a fog come in quickly or a severe snowstorm come on. We dropped anchor a few times sailing through the fiords, and after an hour it would clear up and we would be on our way again.

The mountains looked lovely and peaceful. As we passed a small white painted house only a few yards away the people would give a wave. The next house was maybe miles away, and they were all painted in various colours.

Our next call was not many miles from the North Cape. I believe it was Honingsvaäg, a small town where we dropped the pilot off. We then had to steam along the Great Tundra, along the Murmansk coast. The barren rocks were reddish brown in the falling light and looked as bare as anything could be. It frightened us to think of running ashore there, with not even a gull in sight.

Steaming off the land, the wind got up again and it started to snow. It was pitch dark when I came out on deck to change watch again, and I did not see anything at all during the night. The third hand told me all about the fishing and the bags of fish he had had to open and the different ships that he had sailed in.

76.

In the early morning someone shouted down the hatchway: 'All hands on deck.' We had reached the fishing grounds and were going to shoot the gear and start fishing. On deck I could see ships fishing all around, with the land only about three miles away.

We had not heard of the twelve mile limit then, we were about to fish three or four miles off the land. Lots of small Russian inshore boats were fishing near us.

The trawl was put over the side and we started to tow the net. The skipper came on deck with a bottle of rum and a glass telling us we would not get any more sleep until we were full up with fish and steaming home.

Giving us a full glass of rum apiece, he said if we wanted any more we would have to pay him three pence a glass for it. He had a card with all our names on it. Each glass we had was registered by one small stroke of the pen until four lines, the fifth line making a gate. This went on until we were on the way home–by which time some of the crew owed quite a lot of money.

It was freezing so hard that, by the time that we had a bag of plaice (about twenty boxes) and the third hand had tied a knot in the cod ends the plaice was frozen hard on the deck. The net was frozen, too, and went over the side again in one lump. The fish had to be put away ungutted which meant that they did not make much money on the market.

The radio operator told the skipper that some ships were catching haddocks twenty miles or so from us, so he decided to steam for a couple of hours and catch haddock.

While steaming, we kept our trawl doors hanging outside the gallows, fastened with a large chain around the frame. The ship was rolling about, making the water splash on the doors, the spray freezing at the same time and joining the galley and gallows in one large ice block, We had to heave to and chop all the ice away or the ship could have turned over. We put the doors back inboard.

After fishing for about an hour we hauled and had a large bag of haddocks, not too big and nice fish. After two or three days' fishing I was fed up with seeing haddocks.

I only had one pair of gutting gloves and they had worn out the first day. After three or four days we were full up to the hatch top with fish. Pulling the last of the ice up on deck we put the last of our catch inside the after fishroom hatch and put the ice on top of it. Then we battened all the hatches down with new tarpaulins on top of the old ones, fixed the iron bars around the square hatches, then knocked the large wooden wedges in to tighten the iron bars. Even while doing this heavy seas sweeping the decks washed them away and they had to be renewed time and time again during gale force winds coming home.

During the fishing days we saw quite a few large Russian trawlers towing their trawls past us. We could see the crew gutting in the fish pounds, and some waved to us. Women were among their crew, gutting and cleaning the catch.

We did not get any sleep at all during the fishing. The skipper was in the wheelhouse all the time, sitting in his large chair near the steam steering wheel, which was in the centre of the big wheel making it easy for him to use to navigate the ship. We used the large wheel while steaming, mostly, and the top of the spokes of the wheel were higher than me.

We gutted the fish whilst towing the trawl. The mate and third hand stood in the after pounds, facing forward, the trimmer and deck hands worked in the fore pounds on the port side. After gutting the fish we threw them across the deck; haddocks aft, other assorted fish such as giant size tiger cat-fish, with large black spots and stripes on them, in the fore pounds. Sometimes, Tommy the deckhand, unable to hold the cat-fish to gut, put the mouth of the fish on the wire warp. Then he gutted it, letting the entrails drop in the pound, and flinging the fish across the deck to the forepounds. What a man he was, his arms were as thick as my thighs and he had never been out of a ship for twenty years.

Another fish which was a nuisance was the large monk fish, or angler fish. It carries on its head a large fishing rod, a type of fin, and dangles a very small fluorescent light in front of its mouth. Small fish seeing this light investigate, following the light right into the monk's mouth.

After the cod end is opened, the third hand, holding the ship's rail to stop being knocked over by the weight of fish coming on deck, does not see every fish caught. The deck may be covered with fish as high as the ship's rail and when the ship rolls, many fish return to the sea, to be eaten by the hundreds of seagulls which have been with us from starting fishing.

With the trawl gone overboard, we settled down to gut, trying to touch the deck with our feet, the fish flapping about under our oil frocks, wetting arse and legs. Then maybe you feel the water running into one of your boots, like a bit of ice going down. Trying to reach the deck you might have stood in a monk's mouth, or maybe a tiger-cat has had a bite of your boot. These things happen. Tommy had half a finger missing. He was gutting in very poor light and did not see the tiger-cat's head near a fish he was about to pick up and gut. The fish closed its mouth on Tommy's finger, the large crushing bones inside its mouth just bit through and he lost half the finger. Some of the crews in other ships I sailed in put their feet in old carbide tins.

It was rum-up time again; time passed quickly and it was freezing hell's bells. I kept rubbing the livers on my hands to keep them warm. It wasn't too bad whilst gutting, my hands are hard, but after stopping gutting and washing the fish I'd have to put my mittens on again.

I noticed that the gap between the mast and the rigging was getting smaller. It was freezing harder and the ice was getting thicker on everything; ropes and wires were thicker now. Joey, one of the deckhands, is down the fo'c'sle. Asking what he was doing, the mate asked me to give him a call to come on deck.

79.

Looking down the hatchway I saw Joey near the stove having a crap. When I asked him what his game was he said it was too cold on deck, his arse would freeze, so he had laid some newspapers on the floor and then flung the paper and contents over the side when he came up on deck again. I had told the mate that he was making the fire up and would not be many minutes. I often wondered how Captain Scott and his companions went on, being taken short in freezing weather. I kept remembering what the North Sea skipper told me, when my hands hurt, to piss on them. My hands were sore with haddock rash between the fingers.

The cook was very good. He took the skipper's breakfast, dinner and tea on the bridge during the daytime. At night the skipper called the mate to take over while he went into the cabin. There he'd have a yarn with the chief engineer whilst deciding what to eat for supper. It was mostly cold fried fish, or currant duff left over from dinner, cut into slices.

Dinner time came and went, a half hour break we had for meals. We always had a bowl of soup first, and it was too much for many a fisherman. Being cold and tired, the heat from the bowl made you fall asleep at the table, sometimes head first in the soup.

After dinner, the cry came from the bridge: 'Knock out aft,' and we hauled in the trawl again. When the otter doors were fastened on their cabins we hauled in the iron Dan Lenos (these were half-bobbins at the ends of a trawl used to keep the net wide open), and the large iron bobbins in the centre of the ship came inboard, everyone keeping well clear of them as they fell into the side of the rail. We had to have a mending hook with which to grab the top of the net, first. As the ship rolled to starboard we all heaved on the hooks bringing the cods' ends nearer to the ship's side, the fish going into the cod ends. Putting a jilson hook into the becket and heaving the bag of fish forward to be heaved inboard by the tackle block, the third hand untied the special knot that he had tied before returning the cod ends back again. Asking for the fanny hook (this was a small hook used to aid light loads–e.g. the cod ends–over the side, which was on a small boom from the main mast for light jobs, he took the opportunity to look over the cowhides on the net first, then said: 'Let go!' and we were ready to go astern and fill the cod ends again with fish. The most fish, or bags of fish, I saw in one haul was fifteen bags of cod at Bear Island. We will not see that amount again!

We were all very tired. I remember the third hand holding the tackle in his hands ready to put the large hook into the bucket as the jilson was lifting the cod ends out of the water full of fish. The tackle block was the largest hook on board, with triple wires. The mate was behind the winch driving the large iron barrels as the trimmer heaved on the jilson wire. The skipper, looking out of the wheelhouse, missed nothing and noticed that the third hand had fallen asleep. Shouting at the crew to hold everything as they were, he said: 'Let him have his sleep before you heave again.' After a few seconds the third hand opened his eyes and the skipper told us to carry on working.

During the time the warps were being paid out, the two trimmers would take the messenger hook, which was attached to a long wire, forward from aft after the warps had been stopped and the winch brakes closed. The trimmer would put the hook onto the forward warp and let it go; at the same time a deckhand would heave the hook and wire back again onto the winch drum and it would come up to the starboard quarter, picking up the after-warp with it, tight up to a roller of the ship's rail.

This is when the third hand did the blocking up: the trawl would be over the side and he would put the block on the two warps aft. The skipper would shout: 'Are the two warps spread out?' and is given the O.K. sign.

Then he'd go into the galley, light a fag and have a quick drink of tea–which is forever on the stove, day or night–before making his way to help the lads who, by then, would be gutting again.

It was a very dangerous job, blocking up the two warps, especially during bad weather when the ship's stern was ceaselessly moving up and down. Sometimes, trying to put the pin inside the small hole which held the block down a man would trap his fingers. Many men had fingers crushed by this method and I remember one Grimsby third hand being chopped very nearly in half by the warps going over him in bad weather. He died in a few minutes.

When one warp was seen to be underneath the other one, the skipper would call the mate to heave one up until they spread themselves out like a large V.

Sometimes the otter doors would cable-lay themselves, the strong tides taking them 'over-and-under' one another. Then we had to stop the ship, heave the gear off the sea bottom, and lay and wait for the two doors to part by themselves.

This happened a few times during my fishing experience. This was called, 'gear cable-laid'. All hands would be on deck hoping the doors would spread themselves and clear. Sometimes they did not, and we had to unshackle one end and make a one-ended job, to clear the gear. Then we had to shoot away again.

Sometimes during the time we were pulling the net inboard with our mending hooks, when the weather was particularly rough, huge waves would come at us, taking the net back again and again, perhaps taking the hook out of our hands. The water would come at us, breaking over the rail, and make us jump up to the life rail.

During the three or four minutes standing waiting for the cod ends to be emptied and tied up, I looked at the net freezing over, the meshes getting smaller and smaller and icing up. By the time the cod ends were overboard the net went over in one white lump.

Putting the fish below decks, we rigged half of a cod end near the top of the hatch and fastened the bottom with twine. Filling the baskets with fish as fast as we could wash them, one of the crew teemed the fish down the hatch, counting the baskets to give us an idea how many kits were down there. (A kit was a measure of fish and by weight was about eight stones.) The net was moved now and again to different pounds for the fish to travel down, the water going on the stage draining and being pumped out by the engineers with the engine room pumps. Once whilst moving some fish and picking the hatch bars up, I took my mittens off; I was sweating although it was freezing hard. When I got hold of the iron bars they stuck to my hands, frozen. It was like grasping a hot poker. Throwing the bars down very quickly, I looked at the palms of my hands and a lot of the skin had come off.

I was in a state. The only thing I could do was to wrap some bagging round my hands and make do until we started to steam home which thank goodness wasn't to be long as we were nearly full up with fish.

As the trawl came up with the next haul, there wasn't much left, and the skipper told the crew to stow up, we were to steam home.

Anything movable was tied up and left until we reached the fiords again. In calmer waters we could stow everything neatly, scrub the decks down, and stow the deck boards under the whaleback in the wooden bins provided for them.

The skipper told the mate to send the crew below for six hours until he required the first watch to be taken. The cook would take the wheel for the first six hours, everyone else below. I reckon we would have been somewhere 40° E to 75° N and believe me it was cold. For how many hours or days we had been on deck, all the time fishing, I forget now, but the only time off was for food and rum.

The crew did not say a lot going below. They took their working clothes off, put day shirts and singlets on, and turned in. I fell asleep instantly, to be awakened by the cook six hours later. He had already got the third hand up from aft, but had to shake me several times before I opened my eyes. I thought it was a sheep that I was looking at! It seemed a long time before I came to my senses.

Going aft along the life line that had been rigged up from the barrel of the winch to the fo'c'sle hoodway, I made my way from the galley taking two large mugs of tea with me. The third hand took one of these off me and told me to steer the ship.

Looking out of the bridge's windows into the night, I thought all hell had broken loose. The sky was flashing with different coloured lights all over the northern horizon. One moment a large blue beam appeared, the next it was white . . . red . . . green. It was beautiful and looked quite near to us.

THE AURORA BOREALIS

The third hand, being an old salt and having been to these polar regions many times, told me that the flashing lights were seen very often above 73° N and 45° E when the atmosphere was clear and it was freezing hard. He said that the reflection from the moon was radiating off the ice barriers–but I'm not sure that that is the real answer. But, whatever the cause, once seen, you never forget this sight all your life: different colours flashing all over the northern hemisphere, all in a few seconds

During the summer months, when fishing in the northern regions, the sun shines day and night. The *S.S. Empress of Australia* used to take passengers from Immingham especially to see the midnight sun during my fishing days.

CHAPTER 7

WINTER TIME

COMING HOME TOWARDS THE NORTHERN COAST OF NORWAY we were trying to find the entrance to Varanger Fiords. The snow was coming down very thick and a worried skipper was trying to keep in a correct depth of water which would take us around the mountainous rocks which were above my head as I looked out of the wheelhouse window.

'One hundred fathoms; keep in a hundred fathoms . . . . port a little . . . . starboard a little . . . ' This went on for ages, it seemed, before we came to a very small pier, or what I would have called a jetty. With only a few houses, I believe it was called Honingsvaäg. Here we picked up a pilot to take us through the fiords to Tromsö again. After I had had enough sleep, I spent a lot of time just looking at the fiords. I was fascinated by the views. Sometimes a trawler would pass us, giving the whistle a friendly blow. The crews waved to one another as the ships passed close by.

I had time on my hands, now, to remember the fishing and fish we had caught, to remember standing on deck watching the black ice freeze the ship up in a few minutes, seeing the jilson wires and tackle wires freeze from half an inch to four or six inches thick in a few minutes, to remember the stubble on the crew's faces and their eyebrows turning white with ice, and to remember the birds screaming for the livers that the crew were taking from the fish being gutted. The men would sometimes hold the livers in their hands for the gulls to take from them. Some of the birds were treading among the fish, trying to get to the liver basket. Holding some of these birds, they only seemed to weigh a few ounces.

We carried spare trawl doors forward, but now I could only see blocks of ice. One of the crew shook the rigging and loads of ice came down on deck. Sometimes the two riggings were joined together with ice.

My hands were by now getting better. The old skipper's advice kept coming back to me, I have just thanked him again in my thoughts; it kept the pain out. The skin was beginning to form on my palms again and the haddock rash had cleared from between my fingers. That really had been quite sore.

The crew were becoming more friendly and talking to each other more; wondering what the markets would be like for selling the catch, and what market the skipper will want to land in, How Grimsby Town football team got on, and how the crew's families are getting on. Each one spoke to the wireless 'op' asking him to send a message to their homes as soon as he could hear Wick radio on the wireless. Some of the crew used to take various items in their seabags, the wives or mothers had put various foods in whilst putting their sea gear for a trip, Apples, oranges, biscuits, sweets, chocolate, tomatoes; all sorts ot things were exchanged in the fo'c'sle whilst steaming. Old Tom, who had been to sea for many years, showed me his tomatoes that he had had put in his bag by his family, bragging about the monstrous size of them, asking the cook to save some ham for a special Sunday coming home tea. He would let the cook have some of the tomatoes to give the crew a treat. He put the tomatoes in a large biscuit tin inside his locker, pushing the tin into the ship's side. To support the tin and stop it from moving about, he wedged it with pieces of wood. I saw the tin was full of large tomatoes, packed tightly inside. On the Sunday, coming home, just leaving Tromsö, he took the tin to the galley. When the cook opened the tin, everyone was surprised to see the tomatoes were hardly bigger than the marbles the kids used to play with. He blamed the freezing weather for it. I have not tried to freeze tomatoes for a month, but no one had any better solution for that mystery.

Coming into Tromsö everything was iced or snowed up. No wonder they called it the Paris of the north: women and young men clambered aboard and some of the crew, having been there many times before, had old friends, The skipper and mate went to local homes for a drink, while the crew either turned in or had a look round the town, if it could be called a town. All that I saw were quite a few nice houses, and I noticed that they had a door on all four sides in case of being snowed up, so that it would be possible to use one which was not blocked by snow or ice. There was one small shop that I could see with a sign outside: Colman's Mustard. I heard they used mustard in hot water for bathing their feet, and they thought that the mustard did them good.

A few Eskimos came to the ship, selling whatever they had made in their igloos during the long cold nights. I bought a pair of slippers for my wife and lad, and some small items they had made from pieces of brass they had found washed up on the beaches. I was told they wanted money for stores to take back with them. Some had walked from Lapland, with their herds of reindeer–which had to forage for their own food, swimming across the fiords from one island to another with the Eskimos following behind them. We had to stop the ship during one passage home to let reindeer swim across first; a lovely sight that was too.

Coming home through the south fiords was a sight I'll never forget. Most ships coming through the west fiords, homeward bound, dropped the pilot off at Lodigen or Harstead and left the fiords for the rest of their journey home along the Norwegian coastline. Owing to the weather being very rough the skipper, Parson John, thought if he went home through the south fiords we might catch the market that he had hoped for.

Remembering a very old pilot who once used to pilot his ship quite a lot, he decided to call at the old chap's home and ask for his help to get the ship through the south fiords. We were steaming through a very narrow fiord. I could see several white painted houses on the hill sides. They had lovely gardens and all had a small path leading down to the water, where most had a small rowing boat made fast to a ring bolt or a stake.

Coming up alongside one house, the skipper told the mate to drop anchor. Having the anchor ready at all times, the mate only had to ease the brake from the drum of the winch and the anchor dropped secure. Going astern, we blew the whistle. After a few minutes a small boat left the shore with the old pilot on board. After having a chat with the skipper they both left for the house.

Eventually the pilot decided to take us as far as he could and still get home again, then someone else would have to take us to Kopervik, the last Norwegian port before we could steam across the North Sea to Grimsby.

Anchor aweigh, we steamed through the fiords. The scenery was so impressive that I was awake all day looking at it. Sometimes we came to a pile of rocks that, at first, I thought we would hit: then I could see a black and white circle painted on one rock and another circle on a second rock. The vessel had to pass between these rocks which was the deep water channel. We had to pull the log line aboard in case the fan got wedged between the rocks and parted the line.

We passed between small islands, very close indeed at times. There was a house here and there, always painted in lovely colours, looking very nice among the fir trees with snow and ice everywhere, I remember passing some small boys playing on the bank. We were close enough for them to pelt small stones at the ship gliding close by. Then we were in the open again, no land in sight. I thought we had left the fiords but no, I saw stakes here and there standing up out of the water, maybe ten or twenty feet above the water level. We passed between them. I also saw several ships' masts and a funnel, vessels which had been unlucky, perhaps trying to get through in fog or the darkness.

There were very few navigation lights showing in those days: the pilot had to be good to remember all the different marks and to keep in the deep water channel. Today, I believe it is all buoyed off with lights and fog signals. The pilot took us into Bergen and told the skipper he would have to pay someone else to take us to Kopervik.

We came across the North Sea and landed on the very day the skipper had wanted. I was quickly down to the docks for my poundage (which was 2d in the £1, after expenses had been taken out) and my liver money which was 5/- to the barrel of forty gallons.

Thirty-six hours later we were on the way back again, passing Stavanger and sailing into the west fiords, picking up a pilot again at Lodigen and steaming into Tromsö, icing up again and talking to the friends we had so recently made in Norway.

We stayed in Tromsö for twenty-four hours on each journey. Sometimes we fished for cod–other trips haddock and plaice. Sighting Cape Kanin, on the east coast of the White Sea, we fished about three miles from the coast. The bags of plaice we caught after only fishing for a couple of hours were colossal, the cod ends being made of double twine with approximately two inch mesh were stretched to the limit.

Heaving the bag of fish aboard was quite a feat. I was on the port side when the jilson hook was put into the bag becket: I heaved on the jilson wire on the inside drum of the winch; the bag of fish came forward towards the fore-mast,. The third hand, holding the tackle block hook in his hands, attempted to hook the stronger becket near the rail top, starboard side. After the hook was in the becket, Neuffy, the other deckhand, would heave on the tackling wires whilst I surged on the jilson. Neuffy, now taking the strain of his treble wires, heaved up. I was amazed at the size of the bag of fish coming aboard, caught in such a short time.

We were the only ship fishing in the vicinity, until the wireless operator told other ships about the big catches we were getting. Ships from Hull, Germany, and Russia soon appared and filled their ships up.

Not every bag of fish we caught came aboard as planned.

Bad weather made the job more difficult, and the cod ends, being made of double twine, sometimes caught on the rigging and would split the net before we could pull the bag inboard. The ship rolling could send all the fish back into the sea. This happened many times during my fishing trips, and on other vessels that I sailed in. Nowadays the net is made of stronger nylon and is very much tougher than the old hemp we used to have.

The wires also are tougher today. Many men were injured or killed by ropes, wires, or blocks, parting while being used, especially in bad weather. One third hand, whose job it was to block the two warps together on the starboard side, aft, was working inside the forward warp ready to block the two forward and aft warps on the block. The messenger hook was coming towards the block bringing the two warps together, but the vessel–rolling in the heavy swell–parted the forewire, heaving it and the block, injuring the third hand, who had to be taken back to port for treatment for injuries to his back but he died being brought home.

For the cod fishing, we had to hunt far north in the Barents Sea. Cod has been caught as far north as 80° N. We were about 75° W on the west coast of Novya Zemla. It was very cold and there was not much time to catch fish before the coal was used up.

Heaving the first trawl up we wondering what wouls be in the net. It was full from end to end with red fish. We heaved the first bag aboard, and left the cod line adrift then cast the cod ends over the side: going astern we let all the fish swim out of the net. The sea was littered with red fish with thousands of sea birds diving on them, tearing their entrails out. After about fifteen bags of fish had been let out of the net we scrambled the trawl aboard and steamed further north, leaving the red sea behind us. These fish are named soldiers, or red bream, today. No one had landed any, to my knowledge, so all the ships must have dumped them.

Many bags of small codlings were dumped overboard if the buyers didn't require them. Some ships had brought small codling home to land but they all found their way to the fishmeal factory or 'over the tip', we called it. When you landed two or three thousand boxes of fish and there were no buyers for them–they went 'over the tip'.

What they did with all this lovely fish I do not know to this day. I'm sure it was not all made into fishmeal. The price paid for it covered the ship's expenses and the fishmeal belonged to the trawler owners so they did not lose anything on the trip; only the crew lost on the trip's catch. It was hard work looking after it, gutting it and washing it, putting it down in the fishroom, then packing it in ice. There'd be no sleep for a week or more. We'd be freezing and wet through, and what did we pick up? £1:18s:6d a week with no poundage and perhaps about £2.10s in liver money. We owed for the bond we bought, so we were glad to be out of the docks and at sea, to try and make a better trip with good fish–cod if possible.

Fishing off the Faroes was what I liked best. The fish from the banks are the nicest looking and tastiest fish in the world. The Gulf Stream, running over the Faroe banks, makes all the shell fish, at certain times, full of rich red meat. The haddock and cod thrive on them. Millions of small codling were caught off the south coast, off Sudero, at certain times of the year, full of mussel meat. The fish were that rich you could squeeze the soft flesh in your hands whilst gutting them. Putting the fish away in the fishroom after washing it in the pounds had to be done very carefully. Many a ship had fish condemned when landed at Grimsby, the buyers saying it was too soft to fillet. The large cod off the Faroe Banks were hard as nails, with very large livers like white mufflers when they were taken out. These fish were being caught by W. Butts' Faroe ships, about 1935 I would say. The weather was not good and three of W. Butts' ships wanted to land on the Wednesday market before Good Friday. We all tried to catch some cod for that big sale.

The three ships were *S.T.Salacon*, which I was in at the time, and the others were *Olympia* and *Strephon*.

We all set the log abreast of Sudero, the last lighthouse on the south coast of the Faroe Isles, and steamed for the Pentland Firth–the gateway to the North Sea.

The wind became stronger from the west. Sailing southerly we had the wind and swell on the starboard side; the weather worsening after each watch. We kept our eyes open for hatches coming adrift, and tightened the lifeline over the ship's rail even more. I noticed that the trimmer pulling the ashes up on the port side had made himself fast with a small rope to the ship's casing, until the last bucket of ashes had been tipped onto the deck: the water coming over the rail soon dispersing them.

During my watch on with the third hand, I had my turn on the wheel, the third hand giving me the course to steer by. I could see smoke from the funnels of the other two ships, and sometimes catch a glimpse of their lights during the dark, so we were all doing the same speed by the look of it. Going aft during the night time, I had to keep the galley fire going and make the tea for the next watch on. Gettng on the bridge with two pots of tea in one hand was a feat on its own, with the ship rolling first to port and then to starboard. You had to climb the steps to the bridge door and open it with your free hand, falling into the wheelhouse at the same time: someone always saying: 'Close that f****** door, I hope you haven't spilt any.'

The weather was worse the next day. The waves were that big, all we saw was water whichever way we looked, and me, being only in my first big gale like this at sea, didn't think much to it. The wind was howling and we could hear it rustling through the rigging. The skipper was in the wheelhouse looking out of the starboard window. Every time a large wave came at us he moved his arm to starboard as if to say: 'Wheel over to meet the wave with the bluff of the bow,' which we did many times.

Coming back on watch later I was surprised to see the

skipper still on the bridge; he had been there all day. The seas were very rough with waves forty to fifty feet high. Thinking back today, and watching the surf board riders on the telly, our small trawlers were doing the same thing. Seeing the other trawlers coming home with us during the day time, and running together on the same course, it was possible to look down the funnel of another ship at times when heading into a trough between the waves.

Going now with engines at half speed, we saw a few gulls. The skipper said these were from the Orkneys, and to keep a watch for any land appearing.

Eventually the seas seemed to quieten down a bit, the waves were not so big and we altered course. Laying in my bunk, my right knee was swollen from knocking against the side of my bunk. I had been rolling about whilst asleep and must have banged my kneecap a few times. Coming on deck I saw that we were entering the Pentland Firth, passing Stroma Island, on the north side of us, and coming round Duncansby Head at about twenty knots with our engines doing about eleven knots. Seven tides at once, and you have to come through at the right time, or else! I noticed the trawl was being pulled about by large gulls with white legs, like a big Albatross. The crew told me they were always on the Pentland Firth,

The cook came on deck for his fish, which he was going to cook for breakfast. But I heard him swearing and cursing the gulls who had taken it. We ended up with fried bread for breakfast.

All three ships could now be seen only a few miles apart from each other, their smoke showing for miles. The wind had now become southerly and was slowing us down.

We entered the River Humber early on Good Friday morning, missing the sale day. The firm, W. Butts, sent a telegram to all lumpers to dock these three vessels on Friday morning, landing forty-four score of large cod, plus other fish. We made £777. 0s. 0d, and the other two vessels made about the same—£777 each.

Mr Badon Winters was the cashier at W. Butts, a one-time Mayor of Cleethorpes.

STEAM TRAWLER *LEICESTERSHIRE* January 1938

During one of my trips to the White Sea, we had some very bad weather and many ships got into trouble; in the North Sea, in Iceland, or in the Faroes. We were fishing in the frozen north, near the coast off Cape Kanin, Russia, when we heard the skipper (Parson John) shout to the mate to get the gear aboard: we were going home.

After hearing him say that I believe that I became a few degrees warmer, heaving the otter doors aboard. The skipper told every one to stop work and be quiet, as the radio operator was taking a message from another ship miles away, it said that the Steam Trawler *Leicestershire* had just gone down in the Pentland Firth.

It stunned us all for a few moments. We knew the crew had just changed over that trip, from the Steam Trawler *Northern Chief.* My cousin Harold Simmons (Scotty) was a crew member.

When we came home I went to the biggest funeral I have ever seen in Grimsby.

Many ships have come into Grimsby Fish Docks with fish catches since the Steam Trawler *Zodiac* fished out of Grimsby in 1881.

The old sentinel, the Dock Tower, still standing on the island at the entrance to the Royal Dock, could tell a few tales if it could speak. Although, in a sense, it does speak to all the vessels and crews entering and leaving the port.

* * * * *

During the war I saw many steam trawlers converted to mine-sweepers, patrol vessels, balloon carriers, drifters. We used to call them Ghost Ships, always following behind to pick the pieces up after the working vessels were blown up.

I saw my old fishing vessel, the *S.T. Cedric*, ex T.C. & F. Moss firm, carrying a balloon at Rossyth, Scotland, protecting the Forth Bridge and the naval vessels moored near by.

Hundreds of the smaller fishing vessels were lost, blowing mines up from the sound of their propellors going over the mine which was detonated by sound. There were few survivors from the trawlers sunk doing this work.

I know that many of the well-known North Sea ships had been blown up by mines during the war either whilst fishing or being used on minesweeping duties.

On a plaque fixed to the west side of the tower, it says something like this:

IN MEMORY OF THOSE WHO SWEPT THE SEAS.

CHAPTER 8

REMINISCING—1933

OVER FIFTY YEARS AGO I MADE FRIENDS WITH some Danish fishermen. They used to come to Grimsby every year, fishing in the North Sea from May until October

After landing their catch, the ships were taken out of the fish docks into the Royal Dock and then moored together in the Alexandra Dock. These vessels were mostly owned by the crews and their families.

They stopped in dock for perhaps a fortnight before sailing again; some twenty or thirty vessels sailing together on one tide.

The seiners were well looked after, their cabins and engine rooms were spotlessly clean. All repairs were done by themselves, unless the repair was too big a job. Some of them would go back to Denmark rather than have repair jobs done in Grimsby. The ships were always painted at sea and looked very clean all the year round.

These ships had a water well amidships in which to keep fish alive whilst in dock so that they could have fresh fish every day. Many ships had lines of dried fish hanging about the deck's upper structure. Small flat fish, tied by their tails, washed and salted, were ready for a meal any time required. It was quite a common sight to see these fish hanging around in their home ports, too.

After all the years that have gone by, I still receive a Christmas card from my friend Aage who lives in Frederickshaven on Denmark's northeast coast. The last time I saw him, he was leaving Grimsby in October 1935 to spend Christmas with his parents. I believe about fifty seiners were steaming home, crossing the Dogger Bank, when a squall of wind from the north caught them unawares. Many of these vessels were lost that night, the *F.N. 288* was one, I believe, and the *Ingaborg F.N.* turned turtle. My friend, who was aboard the *Ingaborg*, having his feet caught in the rigging, came back again, having turned over underneath the water. The cook was lost, and Aage lost two brothers. Out of seven brothers, he is now the only survivor.

BIRDS ON BOARD

Whilst we were fishing at sea many different birds came on board, especially in bad or foggy weather. Many pigeons from different countries came to rest on some part of the vessel: they were tired and hungry after flying in circles. Getting into a thick fog seemed to put them off their course for home.

During one trip, as many as ten a day came aboard to rest. The cook looked after them in the small boat aft, feeding and watering them each day until he had fifty or sixty birds in the lifeboat. When we reached the River Humber, early in the morning he would let them all fly away; a lovely sight, just to see them flying towards the coastline, safe.

Many ships I went in looked after the pigeons that came along, saying it was lucky to have them aboard. Some of the crews kept them in a spare bunk in the fo'c'sle until going home, feeding and watering them, and letting them go near the river.

One pigeon came near where I was working and dropped on the deck. Picking the bird up, I was thinking about getting it a drink, when its head just drooped in the palm of my hand. It had died coming aboard. I later took the ring from its leg and sent it to the News of the World, who found the owner, someone in Wales, and told them about their pigeon.

Another lucky pigeon trying to land on board missed the rail and fell in the sea, whilst we were steaming. The skipper, being on the lookout in the wheelhouse, saw this happen, and told the helmsman to turn the ship round and the crew would rescue the pigeon, which we soon had aboard. We found it on top of the water with its wings spread out, keeping it afloat. After a fresh water drink it was O.K.

Many pigeons were saved at sea by trawlers. The birds could see the smoking funnels for miles, and, when lost, headed for the ship.

While fishing in the North Sea, before the war, we laid a buoy down. Towing past the buoy just before dark, I was amazed to see, standing on top of it's flag stick, a great tawney owl with two very large 'ears' sticking up above its head. It was the largest owl I have ever seen. I did not seem to mind swaying about with the tide and wind.

I have seen many sparrow hawks take a bird to the trock of the mast and pick the feathers from it before devouring it, then rest until dawn before flying off to work again. They told me that the hawk helps the flocks of birds migrating to our coast by keeping them off the water, the hawk getting underneath the flock and frightening them to fly upwards away from the spray from the sea, which would dampen their feathers, hindering their flight. The hawk would live on the stragglers.

I saw many chaffinches and goldfinches come aboard, and starlings came in thousands. Settling on anything that a bird's foot could grasp we would see a starling: ropes, halyards, wires, rigging, wireless aerials—everything had a starling on it. But when daylight came they had all flown away.

Another small bird, very unusual, was the golden crested tit. On one occasion the weather was very hot and about twenty came aboard whilst we were fishing. They were tiny birds, weighing almost nothing, flying down into your hands you could hardly feel them. Some birds came down to the cabin whilst we were having dinner, and a few flies were soon eaten by them. The small mushroom airvent on top of the cabin deck soon attracted them and then away they went. I enquired about these birds and was told that they flew from Mongolia with the trade winds. They were tiny and had a gold V on their breasts. The small flies that came aboard were transparent. Their wings had small white stars on them. I have never seen any since that hot day.

COD ENDS (nicknamed by the fishermen: 'The Money Box')

The cod ends are the most important part of a trawl net. Everything comes out of the cod ends. Food, coal, fuel, ice, nets, stores, wages, our rent, kids' clothes, beer money, anything you can think of comes out of the cod ends.

The man who looked after them was the third hand, who, by the way, had to have a third hand's certificate to navigate the ship and be in charge of a watch. A good third hand was like another mate, always the big muscle of the ship. Being in charge of the cod ends was his job alone. If he required any help with them it was always given, no questions asked.

Steaming down to Iceland, weather permitting, he would see all was clear and then leave the deckhand to steer the ship, so that he could look at the cod ends he was going to use for the first haul. If a new pair was going to be used, he would wait until the crew were about to give him a hand to stretch them on deck over the hatches. This would happen at dinner time whilst changing the watch. While we were steaming during the calm weather, an old pair of cod ends would be cut into false bellies, as we called them. These false bellies were the net cut across and about ten meshes down, making a small curtain. It was fastened by using a mending needle, across the bottom of the new cod ends, with another one just underneath, and so on, until half the cod ends were covered, maybe using ten false bellies to cover the new net. Over the top of the false bellies were cow hides, fastened with twine through holes in the hide top. As many as four hides were used to cover the bottom part of the cod ends. New cod line meshes were made by the third hand, and a new cod line which he greased well before he tied them up using a special knot.

All this work had to be done because the sea bottom where we were going to fish had sharp shells, stony ground, needle-like pinnacles, and all sorts of things that could make holes in the cod ends; and we had to try to keep the fish in the net, not lose them. In those days, the cod ends were only made of hemp and it had to be double twine to make them stronger.

Sometimes we would catch large stones, and the stone, bouncing on the sea bed, would travel the whole length of the net making holes in the belly of the net all the way down to the cod ends. Occasionally we lost the stone and all the fish. Sometimes we got the stone aboard and the fish were crushed. We made the stones fast forward, and dumped them coming home, off the fishing grounds. Some skippers asked the third hand to put strengthening wires inside the cod ends.

When the net was being pulled up one day, we saw a bag of whale's entrails caught up inside the net. It took quite a while to get rid of these and the smell was not pleasant. They weighed about half a ton.

I remember one stone coming out of the cod end through the hole that it had made in the net. It fell out whilst the third hand was untying the knot to open the cod ends. This stone fell on his foot, breaking some of the bones. He had to be put into hospital and was off work for a few months.

Tommy Branson, a skipper sailing out of Grimsby, knew how to catch fish—if there were any to catch—in stoney ground, among the hosarses and queen beds. He took me to the river head and we hauled a small trawl he had made out of some lace curtains, and used cotton reels for bobbins, throwing some small stones near the mouth of the net to see what happened, how the stones behaved going down the belly. He showed he how to make a queen trap, or stone trap, so that when towing your trawl and ricking up stones they fell out of the belly before going into the codends and doing any damage. He was very fast mending the net, and showed me how to stretch it out before repairing it.

Some skippers would not use a queen trap, believing that you lost fish out of the large meshes in the belly. But we always believed that the fish went into the net and swam along the top, trying to get out, never going down to escape. Anyway we always had clear fish, none chaffed, while using one.

On another trip, the catch having been spilled from the cod ends, we started to gut the fish. Making my feet feel the deck through the fish that were up to the tops of my thigh boots, I picked what I took to be a piece of brown wood out of the pound to throw overboard. It was not a piece of wood, as I had thought, but was the nose of a walrus which had drowned while we were towing the trawl. We put a becket round it, lifted it over the side with the fanny hook and let it go.

My brother-in-law, fishing in one of Letton's ships, had the same thing happen. The walrus came out of the cod ends, scattering the crew who had to seek shelter from it in the galley. Eventually the crew, using the short hawks (poles which were about twelve feet long and with a hook at the end e.g. boat hooks) to pole at the walrus, drove it overboard by rigging some deck boards to the rail, and the walrus flopped its way back into the sea—but not before biting into the short hawks and snapping the two inch wood into pieces. They were glad to be rid of it.

One voyage, we caught a large whale whilst fishing during very bad weather on the Faroe Bank. We hauled the trawl aboard with this massive tail swinging over the bridge top. You would never believe your eyes, water poured over the rail every time the ship rolled.

We had great difficulty getting a becket around the tail part, but did manage to get the jilson hood through the eye of the becket. We heaved tight, at the same time managing to put the tackle into a second, stronger becket around the thick part of its tail. We heaved tight, slowly. The ship was rolling like a balloon on the wave tops, the skipper, looking out of the bridge window, shouted out orders, telling us what to do and what not to do. I was pulling on the jilson, and the other deckhand was pulling on the tackle wire. Both of us were heaving slowly until all the bobbins came inboard, the head and shoulders of the whale were still outboard.

We could heave no more, The tackle was two blocks together and the jilson hook tight up to the block. Waiting for orders from the skipper about what to do next, I looked up the mast, forward, and saw whale, net, and bobbins, hanging like a large curtain. Everyone looked frightened, what was going to happen next? The skipper, Harold Brennan, who was a good Faroe seaman and knew these dangerous waters, told the mate to fasten the ends of the tackle and jilson wire down, and when he gave the order, we were to let the wires go quickly, allowing the net, bobbins and whale to go over the side. We would chop any ropes or wires, freeing the ship, so we could dodge to safety. The weather was getting worse every hour.

'Let go!' came the cry from the bridge. Throwing my wire off the drum first, my mate threw his tackle wire off a second later. We both jumped clear of the two wires, which were reversing from the drum of the winch at terrific speed.

The whale did not go overboard as planned. It had other ideas. Its head went into the starboard scupper and its tail went over the port side bow, with the middle part on top of the hatches. Net and bobbins now lay loosely around the deck. What a sight! You could hardly believe it possible.

Bringing the ship round into the wind, the skipper manoeuvered it very slowly, trying to keep the water from coming aboard.

First thing was a hot drink of tea, then knives and saws. We stripped all the net off the whale. The ice choppers being down in the fishroom, we got two large fire axes from the skipper's berth. Taking one axe, I gave the whale a really hard hit, where I thought it would split the carcass. But the axe just bounced off, hurting my arm. We had to cut into the blubber before we could axe it. It was a bull whale, the penis being joked about by the crew, very thick and long. It was chopped off and dumped over the side. We were approximately twenty-four hours getting rid of it and washing it down. Dropping our anchor in the harbour of Vestermans Haven, we told the Faroe folks about it and they were sorry we had not brought it with us as they would have had it for food. We mended the net, the anchor watch was set, and we had a good sleep until the weather broke and we were able to leave harbour to fish again.

One day the third hand untied the cod ends. The crew stood by holding their caps or fingers to their noses. The smell from the cod ends!—what was it? Out dropped two dead porpoises, two sea mammals which I think had been laid on the sea bed for quite a while It was the worst smell I had encountered for a long time. You could smell them even after we had dumped them: in the galley, in the cabin at meal times, in the fo'c'sle; for days, the aroma was there.

We had another terrible smell, caught in the cod ends again. It was a net full of herrings a drifter had lost. They were absolutely rotten. When the net was cleared from them we had to shovel and hose them over the side. The smell was awful, even worse, if possible, than the two propoises. Oil from the fish was clinging to our boots and clothes, and many days passed before the stink cleared.

During my fishing life we caught two sturgeon. The cook tried to bake a small one for our dinner. It tasted wooky to me; I did not like it. I think he forgot to put any flavouring in it.

The other one found itself at Buckingham Palace. After it was landed on the pontoon the lumpers made a table out of boxes in the centre of our catch and one solitary fish lay in state. It was sold to Mudd's firm for £35—which was a large sum of money in those days.

We also caught sharks in the trawl at times. They were mostly small but one caused some anxiety as I have already recounted.

I do not think there is much more to tell about cod ends. We used to catch large bags of queens, a clam family shellfish. We shovelled them over the side, making the shovels silver-looking. By the time the trip was up, someone had designed a queen trap to fix just above the cod ends of the belly side, and we could lose most of them that way. Today, the queens would make a lot of money but in those times no one would buy them. The cook jarred some for the crew to take home.

A few years later someone devised a pair of cod ends made from double nylon, which lasts a very long time, saving a lot of money.

1939—MY LAST TRIP BEFORE HOSTILITIES

Having previously joined the Royal Naval Reserve, I had now to report to the Board of Trade at certain times. We were having a day or so in dock so I went to the naval officer in charge, in the Board of Trade offices, who told me to report to him after my next fishing voyage.

At that time I was deckhand of the Grimsby trawler *Edwardian*, one of Butts' firm's ships, and we had just left the dock again for sea, when the mate, telling me he expected some bad weather, told me to mix some sand and cement to put round the cable pipe on the whale back, before the water coming over the bow went down the pipe into the cable locker. Mixing the cement and sand, with a handful of soda and using boiling water, I clapped the mixture round the pipe and cover. It set very hard within a few minutes.

We rigged the lifelines up, fastened the bobbins to the rail, set the log at the Spurn Light Vessel, set the watch, and set off for the coast of Norway again.

It was very choppy at first. During the early morning watch I was looking out of the wheelhouse window when I saw (as I at first thought) a white line of paint from a tin that someone must have knocked over. It was slowly coming towards the scuppers on the starboard side. I told the third hand what I had seen and he said we had no white paint aboard, and would I go on deck to see what it was.

When we put the lights on on the deck we found thousands of maggots which had come from a full basket of haddocks someone had left under the whale back, among the deck boards. We were clearing maggots for several days. They crawled everywhere, down the fo'c'sle, on the sides of the bunks and even on the bulkhead. I did not know a maggot could crawl upside down—but I do now.

We picked the pilot up as usual at Lodigen, and came through the west fiords to the capital of the north, Tromsö. The skipper went off with his friends and we had a few jobs to do, including putting a new trawl on the starboard side. I had taken some things for my friends there such as chocolate, cigarette papers and soap. and we also gave a few meals away. I remember Neuffy, Joey and Tom going ashore.

Steaming through the fiords again, going northerly, we dropped the pilot off at Honningsvaag. Steaming past the Great Tundra, I looked at the barren mountains as we passed, no trees or green to be seen, only reddish-looking rocks, for miles and miles. We fished, this time for haddock, and the bags, coming aboard, filled the pounds so quickly that when the ship rolled the fish were going over the side again in dozens at a time. We were gutting, it seemed, for days on end with no sleep, the skipper, Parson John, came round with his bottle of rum; Big Tommy asking for two tots and the skipper telling him off for having two gates put on his card at once.

I had haddock rash again on the fingers. It seemed this rash came on when you gutted the fish. The sand freed from the entrails had a fine grain to it, bursting when you gutted the fish. This sand got rubbed between the fingers, making them red and sore. After some time they would fester and burst making the fingers stick together. The pain was like toothache and never eased up. All the men involved in the gutting got this trouble—but only with haddocks.

We were glad when the skipper decided to go for some plaice, 'to mix the trip'.

I noticed Joey, who used the fo'c'sle as a toilet during the freezing weather, left three deck boards near the scuppers to sit on; each time the ship rolled it cleared away through the scupper doors.

Catching a nice trip we made for Honingsvaäg again, passing several other ships coming out to catch fish. Arriving at Tromsö we said farewell to our friends, not realising that we were not to see them again.

*   *   *   *   *

We came home to Grimsby and, as instructed, I reported to the Board of Trade. Without further ado I was given my rail ticket to Portsmouth. Arriving at Pompey on the 16th of August 1939, I became X21513A. I was sent, with three other fishermen, to do our R.N.R. training at the Victory Barracks, Portsmouth. It was to be a six weeks course—but it took me until 1946 to arrive back to continue fishing again. During those six years I had been mine sweeping on many different trawlers, many not coming home again.

The minesweeping-trawler crews were all brave men: they had to endure hard work, long hours and trying to kill an enemy who couldn't be seen. Some of the mines were triggered by sound only; some were magnetic; some if you touched them with your bow: and so many more things the enemy had in store: E boats, planes dive-bombing, submarines. Thousands of fishermen died trying to keep the lanes open for our food supply and arms from America. Not only fishermen from Grimsby but men from all over the world. I'd especially like to mention those who had never been to sea in their lives before, who joined the mine-sweeping service and died for the cause.

The Hodson brothers, all seven of them, were skippers out of Grimsby. Frank I met in Granton, Edinburgh. He was skipper of a mine-sweeper. His ship had eleven footballers aboard, and each port he went to, he let them play. I remember him running on the outside line, rallying his crew on, giving them a tot of whisky out of the bottle he was carrying in his hand.

Fred was another mine-sweeping skipper. Like Frank he liked his whisky, too. When a mine sweeper blew a mine up a chevron was painted on the funnel. Fred's ship had more chevrons on the funnel than any other vessel. He would go into a minefield to blow them up.

Charles was the eldest brother, a good fisherman, and Albert was another. Alf was the teacher at the nautical school. Most of these brothers sailed in the North Sea.

I sailed with Frank Hodson as his mate, taking the *Rose of England* for several trips whilst Alf Walker, who was his regular mate, took his holidays, and on another occasion when Alf was ill.

Both these men were well-known skippers, and very respected by their men. They knew all the fishing grounds, and how to fish them. Both skippers died some years ago. People like these are never likely to be replaced.

Some entire fishing families joined the RNR and served—all or most of them—in minesweepers in many different places, at home and abroad.

*   *   *   *   *

My story of the war ends here, I am now on Dobbie's corner, near the Fish Dock bank on Murray Street, waiting for a mate's job.

AFTER THE WAR—AROUND 1947

Grimsby Fish Docks—the first time that I had been there for seven years—I was standing on the corner of Auckland Road and Cross Street, and I was looking for someone to ask for a mate's job on a trawler.

When I had left, some seven-and-a-half years before, it had been really busy, men with barrows littered the roads, taking fish everywhere. I looked around and felt sick; it was like coming back to a ghost town, no Laughing Joe, Little Mick, Cockles, Joey, Squeaker, and many, many more seemed to be in my mind. Were they lost? Were they at sea? I feared the worst.

Coming round the corner I could not believe my eyes: there was the old Stone Wall Ghost himself, Harold Moss of the United Steam Fishing Company and the T. C. & F. Moss firm. The last time I had spoken to him was when we once came into Grimsby for repairs during the war, in a minesweeper. Coming from Hull to Harwich a mine had blown our propellor shaft off its mountings. It was while the repairs were being done that I had met Harold and he had asked me if I had seen anything of his son Peter.

This time we greeted each other and shook hands, but the only job that he had to offer at that time was a third hand's, until a mate's job came by. As it was the only job on offer I took it.

Meeting him the next day, I collected my gear from Dobey's Red House stores and went back to sea fishing again.

The trawler, I believe, was the old *Clacton*, The skipper had been mine-sweeping during the war, but he did not talk about it at all.

After that trip I signed on the *Glen Kidston's* log book and went home.

My wife did not like the long trips, she wanted me to get a job ashore to be at home every night, but I told her I did not know how to work in factories and suchlike after being at sea for so many years. I said that after this trip I would sail in the North Sea, so as not to be too long away.

My bag was packed, my sea gear had been put on board by Mr. Ward who collected most fishermens' gear on the horse-drawn cart he had for the job. I walked over the Humber footbridge to the vessel, now blowing off steam and waiting to leave harbour. When the crew was all aboard, we slipped the moorings and quietly left the docks, the skipper and mate taking the vessel out of the River Humber.

After seeing the lifelines were fast and all movable gear was properly stowed, we all went down to our berths to get shifted, as we called it, into our working clothes. I realised that I only knew two men from pre-war days. One was an old neighbour of mine, deaf Tommy, and another, who lived in John Street (off Victor Street), had a brother who had been a school mate of mine, Tommy Revel. The rest of the crew was unknown to me.

The log was set at Spurn Light Vessel, and the skipper asked the crew to go on the bridge to collect their bond and so on.

As it was August, we had some nice weather. Going through the west fiords again, we picked the pilot up at Lodigen, and headed through the fiords to Tromsö After cleaning all the coaldust out of the fishroom, we scrubbed out the pounds and fitted all the pound boards in place ready for ice to be put aboard. No one seemed to want to talk much. Several boats coming home from the fishing grounds passed by and blew the whistle to us.

We passed the upturned battleship, *Tirpitz,* just a large rusty hulk. There were also several funnels and masts sticking up out of the water, reminding me about the horrible war they had had there.

After several days' steaming past the Great Tundra, someone told me that it was my watch. Coming out of the fo'c'sle, I asked if it was dinner time. The watch told me it was midnight, though the sun was still shining. The crew did not talk to each other much, really only about local news, and never about the war. I learnt that most of the crew had been fishing during the war years and did not like to talk about it.

The fishing was heavy. I had never seen such large bags of plaice come out of the water. We were close to Cape Kanin on the east side of the White Sea. Sometimes the bag caught the rigging, and we lost all the fish. We hauled two hours later and the bag was full again. After the third hand had unleashed the codline, plaice streamed all over the deck, filling every pound. There were hundreds of baskets in each haul.

The crew became very arrogant at times. Whilst gutting, one of them went on the bridge to ask the skipper why he had not brought the rum ration, and struck the skipper a blow for not giving the mate a bottle to share amongst the deck crew. He was a man you kept away from. Eventually the rum was issued and all was O.K.,

I cannot remember who the cook was, but he must have been new to the job. The food we had was enough for four men each. The crew piled their plates four inches high—and they had two helpings. Eventually we had to live on fish for many meals as the cook had used up all the stores too quickly. It was now fish for breakfast, dinner and tea. I usually like fish, but even I was getting a little tired of it!

I remember a few new trawlers from Hull and Grimsby (Yorkies and Grimies) arriving to fish near us, after our skipper had told the wireless operator to give out our position to them, telling them we were on a good living here. Some Russian trawlers passed by closely, their crews waving to us.

The skipper came on deck and told the mate to call it a day and stow up, after icing the fish down.

Steaming towards the North Cape it was a beautiful sight, seeing the mountains as we closed in to the land. Fine weather, sea flat as a pancake, the sun shining twenty-four hours a day. At other times, when it was dark, the Aurora Borealis might be seen and it was more beautiful than ever. Coming closer to the land, the skipper looked for the fiord he wished to enter. Mountains now towered above the ship, which was zigzagging to port and starboard, keeping in the one hundred fathom line, we soon moored at Honigsvaag; one of the northernmost ports in the world. It was not much to see before the war, but now was even less, since the Germans had blown up everything before leaving.

While waiting for a pilot I noticed a young soldier standing on the pier. I asked him if he was stationed nearby. He told me that he had come out of the mountains to the southeast, and was trying to get to his home, on leave, but he might have to wait a month before a boat came. He lived on an island near Lodigen, where we were to drop the second pilot from Tromsö. I asked the skipper if it would be O.K. if I looked after him and let him sleep down the foc'sle.

Calling again at Tromsö we bought a few souvenirs from the Laplanders trading there. The crew were also buying slippers, fur hats and other goods. Tommy was more interested in buying some butter that was going cheap—a twenty kilo box. He borrowed £2.00 from the third hand for this, intending to pay for it from the crew's money when we reached Grimsby. He was going to share the butter between us. After having a row with the third hand, who wanted to keep the butter for himself as he had paid for it, Tommy threw the box over the side as we steamed across the North Sea—so no one got any butter at all. Before that we had dropped the pilot off at Tromsö and picked up another one up to take us to Lodigen where we bade the soldier and pilot goodbye, and left the fiords to steamed across the North Sea for home.

THE CARPATHIAN CAPTAIN

After the war, it was the Faroe fishing that interested me more than anywhere else. One night, whilst sheltering in the fiords from bad weather, when going into the galley to make the tea for the following watch coming on, I saw the cook, a tall slim person, bathing his feet in a bowl of hot water. I asked him if he had hurt himself and he told me a remarkable story about being a captain in the famous Polish regiment, the Carpathian Lancers. The reason he came to sea, he told me, was that the

Russian secret police were after him and his friend, who, he told me, had gone to Aberdeen to fish, so that they were not both together. The feet he was bathing had been frost bitten after walking for miles in the frozen waste.

The poor chap was drowned off the Faroes some time later. The body of this brave man is buried in Scartho Cemetry.

AGROUND

Coming home from the Faroes in the *St. Olympia* we saw a vessel pass us in the dark, returning from Iceland. I cannot remember the name, but I do recall the ship showing the red and green lights at times, that was more than eight points out of his course.

I reported this to the skipper who said we had to keep our eye on it, the crew may have had a drink. At daylight we saw this Yorky ahead of us, but still not making much greater speed than we were, and still yawing a lot.

However, as darkness fell, I saw seven red flares light the sky. We woke all crew to stand by, and went as near to the Yorky vessel as we dared. He had hit the Old Man of Hoy and was fast aground.

At daylight we tried to lift our only lifeboat overboard but all the ropes and wires parted and we could do nothing to help. We saw the Stromness lifeboat arrive and take all the crew off the Yorky. The ship then slipped off the ledge it had been sitting on and sank.

Later I learnt the name of the vessel and that the skipper had had his ticket taken from him for a period of twelve months, the crew having drunk rum and perhaps other refreshments, while steaming home!

CHAPTER 9

BACK TO THE NORTH SEA AGAIN

A s I HAD BEEN PERSUADED TO TRY TO DO I began to fish again in the North Sea.

The Boston Deep Sea Fishing Company had started up on the fish docks. They had two North Sea ships at first, the Steam Trawler *River Spey* and The Steam Trawler *Newlands*. I signed on the *River Spey* as mate.

We fished south of the River Humber around the South Knoll Light Vessel. Towing our gear one morning we hauled, to find about ten bombs fastened together with an electric wire to each nose, painted red and green. I knew they were dangerous, I had seen many during the war.

They were hanging on the bobbins. When the net was cleared from them, I drilled the crew in how we should move each one and carry it to the stern of the ship. We dropped all the bombs at the same time and cleared away from that fishing ground.

As the trip continued the fore part of the ship became littered with pieces of planes' wings, mine cradles and other such litter, which did a lot of damage to our nets and wasted a lot of our time and lost us plenty of sleep.

The fishing grounds were not the same as we had fished before the war. We fished for longer periods, but as soon as we had shot the gear away we caught up on something that hadn't been there before. The pieces of aircraft fuselage we heaped forward as the days went by; bombs were fastened down on loose net, and mines were laid on the rail on net, taken into shoal water out of the fishing grounds and dumped. Magnetic, horn, and many other mines we picked up and dumped inside the limit line. My friend, skipper Charles Halberg, lifted a whole

Spitfire on the rail and took a photo of it. Around the bent propellor were hanging a dozen broken tickler chains. We hooked a set of steam trawler engines with our after warp that had somehow slid between their piston guard on the sea bed. Our ship stopped and hung into the tide, our starboard rail only about six inches from the water. We heaved very steadily on the warps, wondering what we were lifting to the surface. The sea was very calm, the tide was running fast, and we were about sixty miles north east of Spurn Light Vessel. Our vessel was now heeling to starboard very badly. Looking over the ship's rail, we saw this large black shape coming to the surface. We fastened ropes around the pistons. This took a long time as the winch was reversing at times with the weight and tide, and it had to be heaved up again and again before we could make the ropes tight on the gallows.

The gallows was made fast by twenty bolts to the deck, secured by eight more bolts and two bars—one on the gallows and another to the deck. Easing the weight off the warp we released it from the engines. With a loud bang the bolts parted and the gallows went over the side. The engines, taking the gallows with them, sank in a few seconds. Taking a sounding with the lead line we marked our position on the chart, and made sure that we did not fish in that area again. We used our port side for the duration of the trip.

Many decomposed bodies were picked up in our nets. There was no identification of who they were on them, and we'd have to put them overboard again.

Each time we came home, we dumped all the rubbish we picked up inside the three mile limit. We had gone back to fish in all our old fishing grounds, but we never thought that we should have to clear up the grounds first.

The most horrifying haul I can remember was this large, black, shiny, cylindrical object in the cod end. Slowly lowering it on the deck, I realised that this was an acoustic mine that was set off by sound. Several round dials were visible. Looking round, I saw that I was on my own, the crew had disappeared aft. I tried to explain to them that it must be faulty or it would have gone off long before now.

They believed me. Anyway I had my toes crossed as well as all my fingers.

The crew rigged some net on the ship's starboard side, and Alf Walker, the ship's skipper, helped us. We spliced new three-inch rope round the mine, making a becket in the middle of it—the mine being six to eight feet long and as far round as a large wooden beer barrel. The crew were sweating, and so was I. I was thinking of the man who had rendered the first mine safe, then got killed by another one.

Making the mine fast to the starboard side, as tight as we could to the net, we steamed back to the fishing grounds again.

Another vessel, fishing nearby, brought a horned mine up in the trawl. Keeping it on deck, the engineer used a spanner and a hammer to take a spike off the mine. Carrying it into the engine room and locking it securely in a vice he started to take it to pieces. The part exploded, severely injuring him and taking his hand off.

Wacka Wakefield had a bit of luck in his ship. Three mines hung in the headline when they hauled and they had to chop the gear away.

One skipper I sailed with—Dick Ford—was tickler chain mad. How the ship got through the water amazed me. One chain was on the bussom, another from the first ten feet of bobbins, and one from the thirty feet point, another from the doors and one from the Dan Lenos. Five or six chains were dragged through mud and sand. We had many fastenings with these chains pulling all sorts of junk up with them from the war. It seemed never to end. Dick Ford had been wounded at the evacuation of Dunkirk and had had a metal plate put into his head by the Germans. He was a prisoner of war until released by the Yanks.

Many fishermen are trying to claim compensation for loss of earnings today. I have often wondered why the government did not compensate the North Sea fishermen for clearing the North Sea of all the rubbish left on the sea bed from 1939 until 1945.

Another skipper I sailed with was nicknamed Hossarse Bill, because he fished amongst the see urchins, which always seemed to cling to any stones or pieces of wood. We would catch a bag of these creatures every haul.

I remember we had been fishing south of the Dudgeon Light Vessel when one of the crew told me he believed the cook was going to knife the skipper. We saw the cook on deck and the skipper trying to keep clear of him. We tried to reason with him, and eventually got him in the cabin, aft. He still had the knife and was going to use it on anyone now. The ship was brought about and we made for Lowestoft. The police, having been informed, came aboard and went to see him. His knife was taken from him, and the sergeant asked him to come ashore. After turning around to climb the ladder out of the cabin, the cook struck a blow at the police officer with another knife he had hidden under the seat locker cover. He missed, and with a little persuasion, the police took him away. I believe the war had something to do with his case. We never saw him again.

When we were landing our fish I used to be on the bell ropes, pulling the fish out of the fishroom in baskets. The lumpers then swung the basket full of fish onto the landing boards where our trimmer stopped it, unhooked the chain hooks, and let them go back to the hatchway man. The trimmer then pulled the basket of fish ashore where the lumpers sorted it and laid it on the pontoon. If cod, it was packed in scores (that is in twenties); skate was packed with the largest on top of the marker and the smallest size was on the bottom; flat fish were packed in boxes.

After it was all landed we went home.

I went home over Riby Square crossing, sometimes going into Riby Square public toilets for a bath, and then across the road to the barber, who was named Jack Death, for a quick shave. These toilets in Riby Square were regularly used by fishermen, as very few had bathrooms at home. There were many public baths in those days.

Going home, I cut through Kent Street, round Bridge Street Station, into Church Street, then into Oxford Street and home. In Church Street an old lady stood in her doorway as I passed by. I would greet her saying: 'Hello, Mrs.,' and she'd say to me, 'I'm still waiting for him to come home.' I knew she meant her son who was lost off Harwich, during the time that I was minesweeping. I remember his ship blowing up one night and all hands were lost.

As the years passed by I had seen her still waiting for her son, many times, until she passed away.

After another trip, when I was on the dock for my wages, a young chap stopped me in Fish Dock Road. He asked me if I knew where he could get a deckhand's job. As we were going to sea the next morning and wanted a deckhand, I told him to call at the Boston firm and ask to sign on the Steam Trawler *River Spey* as deckhand. The rain was pouring down, he had an overcoat on, wet through, and a case with a few belongings inside. I told him to live on board until we sailed and wait to find lodgings until after we landed from the next trip. Going on board the following morning, I was surprised to see him up and ready to sail. I told him he would be in my watch, and we sailed to the fishing grounds. During the watch he told me he had come from Aberdeen, and had been sailing out of the Deen for some time. His name was Jimmy Donald.

We had a lot of mending to do to the trawl, which had split each haul as the result of the usual problem of the net catching on old wrecks or the debris of the war. Whilst I was mending the net, the third hand was on another job, doing his cod ends, and I asked Jimmy to mend a large hole in the square. To my surprise he mended the hole very quickly, and whilst we worked together he was mending as quickly as I was; and I was fast at mending! I had had some good tutors.

A trip or two later Jimmy came third hand with me, after telling me that he had a third hand's certificate from Aberdeen. The firm bought a trawler named the *Dunsby* to fish in distant waters. Jimmy asked me if he could sail in the *Dunsby*. I talked to the ship's runner and he gave Jimmy the job, taking my other deckhand with him.

Whilst fishing in the White Sea, Jimmy's back was badly burned, and the deckhand who went with him had his leg trapped in the bollards, the warp cutting through the bone. Jimmy had to cut the deckhand's leg free, and rush him down to the cabin, putting the stump of his leg into a bag of flour to stop the bleeding. The skipper tried to go into a Russian port with him but was refused entry. They took him to Norway and saved his life.

Jimmy Donald sat for his mate's ticket and became mate of the biggest trawlers of Boston Deep Sea Fishing Co. Later he became skipper of them, taking every new ship he wanted. Where he finished up I do not know, but what a fisherman!

Still sticking to the North Sea, I sailed in several ships belonging to T.C & F. Moss, that had survived the war. The crews consisted of American soldiers who had stayed in England hoping to get used to fishing; a few miners who wanted a change of scenery; and a very large number of men who eventually became plonkies on Riby Square.

The crew, fighting each other on deck, became a nuisance. The skipper asked me to stop them, but I told him to let them alone to fight each other. If we interfered they would turn on us, so we watched. I told the skipper that after knocking hell out of each other they would be the best of pals later, and so they were.

There were no better fishermen, before they became plonkies. I knew most of those who ended up in Grimsby, and there was always a story behind each one of them who turned out that way.

One man's story that I would like to tell. We were fishing at the Faroe Isles, one cold dark night, and the wind was blowing hard. I was on watch, towing the trawl and looking out of the starboard window. I saw the big rollers looming in the dark, a big white top crashing onto the deck every now and then. Tommy came in the lee side with two mugs of tea. You could see the steam from the mugs, it was that cold. I said to him: 'There's some heavy swell on this side,' to which he replied: 'There is some on this side too, come and look.'

Going to the lee side and looking out of the window, I saw about twenty large black fins, four to five feet out of the water. It took me some time to realise these were basking sharks, very big ones too. They stayed alongside for about half an hour and then left us.

Back in Grimsby while we were mooring up in dock, it was a custom to take the warps off the drums to be remarked by the wiremen, who worked both ashore and on trawlers in dock, resplicing and marking. We cabled the wires on the port and starboard quarter deck. As we were doing this, I saw a woman looking at the ship from the quayside. She was dressed in black and, for some reason, I thought she might be some relation to Tommy.

I told him someone ashore might be looking for him, and to take his sea bag with him and not worry about coming back now, we could manage the job without him. We did not see anything of Tommy during the landing of our catch, either.

Later I learnt that while we had been at sea, Tommy's six year old son had been killed and buried without him knowing. The skipper was supposed to have received a message from another ship that had come to the Faroe fishing grounds from Grimsby, asking the skipper to transfer Tommy to a ship returning home, so that he could attend his lad's funeral. This was not done.

The only times that I ever saw Tommy after that he was with the plonkies of Riby Square. After each trip, the crews gave him a few shillings, but it all went on booze.

Sometimes some of the plonkies decided to go to sea again. First one would go for one trip, then another would go for a trip. They shared the wages and settling between them.

It seemed odd to me that the skipper who was supposed to have brought Tommy home later fell overboard and was drowned. Tommy died a few years ago, a great plonky and shipmate.

CHAPTER 10

'

THE STORMY PETREL AND OTHER MEMORIES

AFTER FISHING IN THE NORTH SEA FOR TEN TO TWELVE DAYS the wind started to blow very hard from the west. We decided to go home, with the weather worsening we headed for the Humber Light Vessel. It was very dark and spray was coming over the bow as we entered shallower water. Looking out of the wheelhouse, I heard a loud bang on the glass and, I thought, a little squeak.

Pushing the wheelhouse door open I looked in front of the verandah and saw a small bird huddled up in the rain and wind. Picking it up, I took it into the wheelhouse and put it in a mug rack, where it lay as if dead.

It was after we'd dropped anchor at the Burcombe buoy that I remembered this bird and had another look at it. I was very surprised to see that it was a stormy petrel, and I also knew they did not normally come this far south. Keeping it warm until daylight, knowing I could not feed or water it, I let it go. It flew away towards the Yorkshire coast.

While I was at home I thought about this bird and wanted to know why it was so far south. I wrote to Peter Scott and, in his reply, he told me that at the time I found this bird a northerly gale had swept hundreds of them from Rockall and the Western Isles, as far as the Bristol Channel, where a westerly gale had then taken over and swept the birds over England into the North Sea. Many stormy petrels were found in the streets of London and right across the country, all dead. He mentioned that not many birds were left on the islands after that gale.

* * * * *

We occasionally caught a salmon in the trawl, the skipper having the choice to take it home if he wanted it.

On the way home from one trip, we had a haul among the stones, hoping that we might lose the trawl, which was very old. If we returned and the trawl was still hanging on to the bobbins, the firm would not give us a new one, only if we lost it would it be replaced. So we tried. We heaved the bobbins aboard, and the only part of the net we brought up was the cod ends, fastened to the belly lines and the lazy decky (a spare rope on each quarter of the net–used to help to pull up the cod ends).

Getting the cod ends aboard was a long job. However we heaved them over the rail, the third hand loosening the cod lines, and the stones came out, not one fish among them. The trimmer threw the stones back over the side, and said: 'Don't you want that?' pointing to the largest lobster I've seen in my life. It was in the ship's side, partly covered by stones.

Retrieving this monster of lobsters, I held the back of it in my right hand and carried it so that the skipper, engineers and cook could have a look at it. As I carried it aft the two big claws dragged on the deck. The skipper told me he had to boil it in the copper in his wash-house at home.

Some time later, when the cod ends were opened, out jumped a fish that looked rather like a haddock. We would have thrown it over the side but, looking at it again, I thought I would ask the Fisheries people to tell me the name of it, as I saw spikes on its dorsal fin.

When I saw the Fishery chaps on the pontoon measuring our catch to see if we had caught any small fish, I showed them the fish and asked them the name of it. They could not tell me, and asked me to let them take it to find out. I agreed as long as they would let me know what they found out.

During the day, the office I sailed for had a phone call asking if it was alright to send the fish to Lowestoft, as no one in Grimsby recognised it. Some weeks later I received a letter from Lowestoft, enclosing one pound, with a slip of paper telling me it was a Black Sea wrasse–the first one brought into Grimsby.

* * * * *

The old *Vascama*, skippered by Tommy Spall, who did a marvellous job during the war, brought back a few memories to me. Signing on as deckhand, I thought I would like a change from catching bombs, planes, etc, and would see a few fish for a change.

Streaming the log at the Spurn Light Vessel we set course for the Vestfjorden, calling at Lodigen for a pilot, then on to Tromsö for our usual ice. Having cleaned the fishroom of all coal dust we washed the fish pounds clean, shipped pound boards in place and took our ice. Taking another pilot we steamed through the fiords to Honingsvaäg where we dropped him off on the pier. Not much of the place left now, I thought.

Steaming along the Great Tundra again, I shuddered to think about running aground on that barren land. Coming up to Cape Kanin we shot our gear. Small plaice were in abundance, but no one on the market wanted them. Too many ships were being built now and only the best fish would bring a good price, especially cod if we could find any. We had to catch our trip in the shortest time possible because the coal did not last long enough for us to spend time looking for fish a thousand or more miles away from Grimsby.

The skipper steamed further north looking for cod. After hauling several times our bag was full of small codlings. The wireless operator told the skipper the fish would only go over the tip if we took them home, so we booted many through the scuppers for bird food.

Steaming towards Nova Zemla, 75° N., the wireless man heard of a German trawler catching cod there. I could smell ice, and the cold, but the weather was good, the sea flat. We shot away, hauling about one hour later to see the trawl come up full of small whales. Getting the first bag aboard we put a rope round each one's, tail, and heaved it over the side with the fanny hook. Neuffy, a powerful deckhand who was sailing with us again, tried to throw them over the rail, but had to give it up. Shooting away again we caught more and more whales. During the day we heaved five large ones over the side, by using the fore and aft warps on them, taking the head and shoulders aft, the fore warp taking the tail part at the same time. I counted one hundred and twenty mammals we had caught, and no cod.

Shooting away yet again, we hauled to see the trawl full of large cod. After fishing for nearly three days and nights without a sleep, we pulled the last of the ice up on deck, filled the hatch to the deck level, packed the ice on top of the fish and battened down. We were on our way home.

After calling at Honingsvaäg and picking the pilot up again, we called at Tromsö. Passing the *Tirpitz* and Lodigen again, we finally made for the Humber. Clearing the Norwegian coast, we came into some bad weather, the wind was north-east, right up the ship's stern. During my watch on the wheel, the skipper came and looked at the log book which we had to fill in each watch with the speed we were travelling, miles per hour on the log clock, wind direction, the time, and anything we saw whilst steaming.

The skipper said that at the speed we were going it would be impossible for us to catch the tide he wanted for landing our fish. I replied that if his father was skipper of this ship, he would catch the tide.

Looking at me he replied: 'How on earth could my father make this ship go any faster?'

Knowing his father to be a bit of a devil-may-care chap (and his brother Arthur too) I said: 'Rig a sail up, and it will make us a mile an hour or more faster than we are going now.'

'How do we rig a sail up? We don't have one,' he said.

'Rig the awning we use to keep the sun off the deck as a mainsail, and let the mizzen out into the wind,' I told him.

He did not open the wheelhouse door but jumped out of the

wheelhouse window, called the day man out to find the awning which we kept in the fore dill (a sink in the fish hold to collect water before it was pumped out). Rigging it to the jilson it was heaved tight and made fast to the bridge verandah by a strong line. The mizzen mast was very soon pulled up and the davit, or boom, swung out and also made fast. Several trawlers passing by to the fishing grounds wirelessed us to say they thought we were a large sailing vessel. We had a heavy list to port, going home.

We reached Spurn Light Vessel two hours before high tide and landed our fish on the day the skipper wanted. All the fish were sold.

ANOTHER MEMORY

Once during our early morning fishing watch, we were looking out of the wheelhouse window. There was an early morning mist. We were fishing off the Smith's Knoll, south side, when seven red lights appeared on the port bow. Seeing these, I altered my course so as to pass red light to red, wondering what it could be. I had never seen seven sailing ships together, I thought.

Getting closer, I could see that the two first reds were on top of each other and the other five lights were in line. I was still scratching my head until I realised that it was a tug towing five barges.

The old herring luggers had to be watched very carefully. While steaming, their forward white light (a paraffin lamp) would blow out and not be noticed by the watch. I passed several luggers with no lights visible whilst steaming, and missed them with little time to spare, pulling the wheel over to pass them, while their nets were down, fishing for herrings.

STEAM TRAWLERS: DISCHARGE RECORD PAPERS.

Before the war, after signing off from a ship you could ask for a discharge sheet. This was given to you from the office, by the officer in charge. It was about six inches by four inches, with a seal on it. It gave the dates that you signed on and off and it gave you a character reference.

When the Record Office opened after the war each fisherman was given a blue book with his ship's name, the date he had signed on and off were stamped on it, and a character reference too.

As time goes by, the fishermen of yesterday may require a record of sea service they did for different organisations, they may not have had the discharge sheets given to them, and now it was too late as the records were lost during the war.

So the records seem to start only from 1946.

It seems very odd to me that many men receive cash aids from various funds, but a lot of old fishermen received nothing; yet they did the same time fishing.

AND ANOTHER MEMORY BEFORE THE WAR

I was walking along the North Wall when fifteen ships came into Grimsby from Germany. Talking to a chap who said that he worked for Marr's Company of Fleetwood, he told me that if I wanted to sail out of Fleetwood in one of these new trawlers, I should contact him there, and I would be shipped up.

The fifteen ships were named:

Northern Spray	*Northern Jewel*	*Northern Gift†*
Northern Rover	*Northern Isles†*	*Northern Sky*
Northern Wave	*Northern Princess†*	*Northern Reward*
Northern Pride	*Northern Duke*	*Northern Return*
Northern Foam	*Northern Sun*	*Northern Dawn*

†These ships at least were lost during or soon after the war.

126.

Painted all white, they looked a picture. They said the ships were in lieu of a payment owed to Lever Brothers.

Also built were six 'fighting ships' for Sir Alex Black, they were named:

S.T. Daneman	*S.T. Italia Ceacer*	*S.T. Man o' War*
S.T. Fighter	*S.T. El Capitan*	*S.T. Le Tiger*

I did not sign on any of these big ships. The North Sea was for me now. I could be home in ten days or less. Billy Blythe was skipper in the T.C. & F. Moss firm; I knew the crew of his ship *Coniston*, and signed on as mate with him again. The old ship was a good sea vessel and could stand the bad weather. We fished in the Silver Pits, on the edge of the rough ground and the hills. Sixty to a hundred miles was the limit with him.

Sometimes, when the cook had turned in for the night, Bill would bake a batch of bread for him, and sometimes just before we returned home, so that the crew could take one of his loaves home with them. Beautiful bread and cakes he made for us. The first sitting for dinner time was from 12.00 noon to 12.30 p.m., the second sitting 12.30 till 1.00 p.m. Skipper, mate, third hand, the engineer off watch, and one decky, were at the first sitting. At the second sitting, the engineer off watch, one deckhand, the cook and trimmer had their meal. The skipper tried to haul, if possible, at 1.00 p.m., 5.00 p.m., 9.00 p.m., 1.00 a.m., 5.00 a.m., and 9.00 a.m..

Many times during the fishing our gear would be caught up on some obstacle on the sea bed. This altered the times for hauling. The cook and engineers did not like the times of hauling the gear to be changed as the cook already had to prepare the food to suit two different times, and the crew would be working on deck until the trawl was fishing again. If we had fish to gut in the pounds on the deck when the cook shouted: 'Dinner up', one deckhand went on the bridge to take the wheel, one engineer had to be down in the engine room, and one trimmer would stay gutting fish, the rest of the crew having their dinner.

The trimmer was old Campaign Smithy who was a great character in T.C. & F. Moss's firm, but he had to be watched very carefully when left on his own on the deck. Coming back from the cabin after having our meal, ready to help to gut the fish, we might find the deck pounds had been lifted up and every bit of fish, shells, and guts, had been hosed through the scupper.

When we asked old Campaign where the fish was he would reply: 'Bird seed, bird seed'. That was all we heard from him. After the first time that happened someone had to stay behind with him, or send him for his dinner first.

What with Campaign Smithy and Military George, the cook, we had a right old pair to watch. Many a time we would go for our dinner after being at sea longer than usual and Military would put a very small dinner on the table, minus knives, forks and spoons. When we asked where they were he would reply that he had accidentally lost them overboard in the washing up water. That was to tell you, in his way: 'Go home–no food left'.

Another character was a third hand who would take your knife if you left it for a couple of minutes. When mending the trawl on one occasion I put my knife on the winch end, on top of the pistons, while I went for my meal. On coming back I asked the deckhand where my knife had gone. He said the third hand had been mending near where I had been, he might have taken it. When I asked the third hand for my knife he asked if that was the only one I had got. I said that it was. Going to his bunk he brought a box of about six inches by four inches, full of knives. I pointed out him my new one, which was marked, in his box. He gave me two more and told me to keep my knife in my pocket in future, where did I think he had got these from.

Bill Blythe was a good North Sea skipper, liked by everyone he met. Not one seaman would say a word against him. At sea he wore a dopper–which was a garment that came over the head and shoulders and down to the ankles. It was made of tough flannel, the same stuff as 'fearnoughts' (trousers) were made of. Billy's dopper was green with age; it had seen more salt water than a lot of fishermen had sailed in. He was never without it at sea nor on the dockside.

Coming home one trip, the wind dropped to nil and the fog came in very thick. We felt our way up the river until we heard the Burcombe buoy's bell, dropping our anchor to the south east of it. We rang our anchor bell now and again if we heard another vessel passing or coming too close.

The *Brenda Fisher*, the selection tug, crawled alongside to tell us we would not be going into dock, as the water was too low to open the gates in the lock pits. We would have to stay at anchor. Billy told the tug skipper that he would like to go ashore, and asked if he would take him into the Royal Dock Basin, The skipper told me to bring the ship in at midnight and said that he would meet us on the quayside.

Midnight came, but the section tug found us again and said that we still had to stay where we were, there was still no water to open the gates. Four tides went by before the gatemen could open them. Though it was still thick fog I found the entrance to the lock pits and moored up in No. 1 Dock. Billy came aboard saying that the tug had not been able to find us in the thick fog, to put him back on board. But he had been seen in the town and word got back to the office, so Billy was told off for leaving his ship.

He liked a little flutter on the horses. Whilst in dock he asked me and my wife if we would like a run out for the day to Scunthorpe. We went by taxi, Billy and his wife and myself and my wife. Stopping at the Black Horse, I believe that was the pub's name, in Wrawby, we went in for a drink. The first words I heard were: 'Hello, Billy, what are you backing for the National?' He replied in his loud husky voice: 'Your horse of course, Sheila's Cottage'. This was in 1948. Wherever Billy went, in Brigg, Scunthorpe or Grimsby, he put money on Sheila's Cottage. How or from where he got his information I do not know. I was serving in another ship when I heard that Sheila's Cottage had won at 66 to 1.

Billy bought a taxi firm with the money he won. He put a lot of money on with various bookies, and some of them he never saw again. So, after a couple of years, he was back at sea again, fishing. Bill Blythe's home was in Cleethorpes Road. The name outside his door was *Jonquil*, a trawler's name.

The steam trawlers *Cedric*, *Gurth* and *Ivanhoe* belonged to the United Fishing Company, managed by T.C. & F. Moss. Jim McCann was skipper of the Steam Trawler *Cedric*, and had been for many years. I sailed with him for quite a while, a nice quiet man who liked to help on deck with the mending and hauling in the trawl. With a two-foot rule he would measure the tickler chains to see if any of them had stretched. If they were too long he would cut a link out until the chain was the exact measurement that he wanted it to be. He would also pull the warps off the winch to measure them if he thought the trawl was not working properly. He, like Billy Blythe, worked the hills for good hard fish.

Harold Maran and Charlie Halberg, also fished for the best, even if they were catching only a little they stuck there. The *Clay Deeps Ghost*, which fished for T.C. & F. Moss, had to stay and wait for the fish to set in, even if the skipper caught very little. The fish, always being good, had their own buyers to whom Tom Moss sold at a good price. Tom (junior) was cashier and salesmen and always liked to see the fish well looked after.

The emblem on these United ships was black and white diamonds on top of the funnel. T.C & F. Moss had a brown and yellow funnel with a black top and with a horseshoe on the funnel.

I can remember being in the *Cedric* in thick fog, coming into the lock pits, listening to the horn blowing on the east pier. We came straight into the Royal Dock Basin. Seeing the top of the Dock Tower, we circled round and came straight out again, not touching anything, going through the Fish Dock lock pits and mooring up for landing. Many times the *Cedric* came in on a Sunday, landing on Monday and away Monday night or Tuesday morning. We did not have many hours in dock before we were fishing again. We had to settle up every three trips, my wife receiving £5 per week allotment.

Coal, ice, repairs if any, food, stores; it was less than £100 per trip. We had to make £200 for a deckhand to pick up £1.13s.4d, which was a good trip those days. The skipper's share was £10 to the £100 and the mate's £7.2s.6d in the £100, after the expenses were taken off. So, if you were lucky, you paid your way. The skipper and mate had to pay for their own food. I believe the Bosun was the best paid man on board ship at 4d in the pound; the Chief Engineer the best weekly paid man.

Whilst I was fishing out of T.C. & F. Moss's firm, I sailed in most of their ships with men who had been with the firm for many years. It was nothing to hear from some members of the crew that they had been with the ship fifteen or twenty years, only stopping ashore if taken ill, or if the ship had had a re-fit. Some of the employees on shore had been with the firm many years too. Alf, the foreman lumper, was the stores man who would put your stores on a barrow and wheel them round the dock to your ship, wherever you might be.

The *Pearl, Diamond, Coniston, Castleton, Clacton, Clifton, Gurth, Cedric, Prince, Leo*, were all out of Moss's office, very old, but very good sea ships. All have since been scrapped, or lost, many years ago. I joined the Royal Naval Reserve whilst serving in these ships, and that was when I met a young chap called Tommy who was a tubey or boiler cleaner for T.C. & F. Moss. He joined the Royal Air Force Reserve, and told me he would one day fly a plane past us if we were anchored in the river on a Sunday morning.

Some time later, coming into the river from a fishing trip, we dropped our anchor off the Burcombe Light Vessel. I was clearing the deck when a plane flew past very low, just above the water, the pilot waving to us, the plane then gave us a salute by dipping its wings up and down. It was Tommy and after landing our fish and putting our fishroom boards down the hatch, Tommy came aboard and asked me if it had been me who had waved back to him in his plane. I told him that it had been and we had a good laugh about it.

For many more Sundays he came and waved to me as he flew past. I missed him when I went into bigger ships and different firms. The war came and went but I never did see Tommy again. I was minesweeping and he was in the Air Force. I often thought of him during the war and then I saw his photo in the Grimsby Evening Telegraph on Thursday 16th 1989. It read: 'Story of a Cleethorpes' war hero.' His name was Tommy Price. He also served on the railway tugs, being a friend of the Marlow family.

The cooks on the trawlers had their share of troubles too. The watchman lit the coal fires in the galley and the cabin, and they were kept alight from leaving the dock until returning. Whilst at sea, the watch on early morning duties cleaned the ashes out and, if necessary, rekindled the fires and one in the fo'c'sle too. We had a ship's tin made fast by iron bars, full of hot water at all times, for washing up and so on. The large tin kettle on the stove was always full and kept on the boil for our tea, which was made and ready to drink at all times of the day and night. The kettle was always secured in place, because the vessel was rolling about all the while at sea.

After our first haul, we would take half a basket of fish to the cook who cleaned it for breakfast, and maybe also for tea time, but we never had fish for dinner. The deckhand on watch during the night sometimes cleaned the fish for breakfast, especially if there were a few gurnards among the catch. We would have plum duff or suet pudding every day after the meal, with custard–as much pudding as could be got on a large plate.

Some cooks I sailed with only had one leg. You would

wonder how they got up and down the steep ladder to the cabin from the galley so many times a day. During bad weather the cook would put vegetables and potatoes in the small boat, aft, to keep fresh and cool; then quite often he would have to ask the watch to give him a hand to fill a bowl up for dinner, as with the ship rolling and tossing about he could not climb inside the small boat for the vegetables. Sometimes the cook, losing his balance, would grab for the galley rail or door, and lose the washing up bowl overboard. Many times I have given the cook his bowl back, after the trawl had picked it up again and it had been found in the cod ends.

The cook fried bread and fish every morning for breakfast. During bad weather we had to keep our distance from the galley. We could hear the swearing and cursing going on, as he tried to keep the fish in the pan. A cook who knew the drill knew how to stop the fat rolling over onto the stove. After breakfast, dinner was prepared. After dinner the cook would turn in to his bunk and have a sleep until the engineer called him to make the tea for us. After tea he would bake some bread and cakes. Some cooks made lovely loaves, sometimes baking a loaf for us to take home. One of the best cooks we had was Old Pikey. He cooked all the shell fish for us, queens, prawns, crabs, whelks, and lobsters, to take home.

I remember coming home from the White Sea. We had a long voyage and most of our food had been eaten so we were having fish of a different kind for three meals a day: fish for breakfast, fish for dinner and fish for tea! Coming home through the fiords we called in at Tromsö, and laid alongside the Grimsby Steam Trawler *Epine.* Harold March, my old school pal, was cook on it. I had not seen Harold for a long time. When I told him that we had had fish for many days he said that he had just made some bread buns and would make us some ham sandwiches. Harold stuttered a lot and you can imagine the difficulty he had telling me in his excitement at meeting together again after such a long time. Our cook went ashore and bought some reindeer meat, which we had while steaming home–and very nice it was too.

The *Epine* was lost later on, fishing off Iceland in 1948. My old mate was with it, also several more neighbours from my street.

Another cook who sailed with me, and only had one leg, used to wear a stump strapped inside his trousers leg. At night time he would remove his trousers with the wooden stump still inside. Getting up in the morning he would pull his trousers straight on, fasten the belts up and he was O.K.–until one of our crew took the stump out of the left trouser leg and fixed it into the other one while the cook was asleep.

I can still remember the cursing, swearing, and threatening to kill the man who did this to him. We kept clear of him that day, making do with a supper after he had gone to sleep again. Next day he just laughed and asked: 'Was your dinner O.K.?' What he put into it we never did know.

If the cook had too many men in his galley preventing him from doing his work, he would drop a pinch of pepper on the stove top. We sure made our exit fast: the smell was choking.

Another cook we had was called Snowy. He was as black as jet, with white hair. He never said much to anyone, and we never knew where he came from or anything about him. He lived in the Mission, and just did his job; he was a very good cook and was obviously well educated by the way he spoke. I did not see him after the war.

We caught many large cockles in the net during our fishing, but shovelled them back over the side. Some of the crew would open them with their gutting knives and swallow the contents alive, saying they were like oysters. We caught these off the Russian coast, off Cape Kanin.

Whilst I was fishing in the North Sea, we trawled in many fishing grounds, the skippers using the lead line many times during the day, to find the ship's position. The electronic navigation instruments used today were not known about then.

I remember the names of some fishing grounds such as Bruce's Gardens, (some nice plaice from there), the Turbot Bank,. Clay Deeps, Haddock Bank, Among the Dutch Farts, Red House, The Steps, Skate Hole, Yorkshire Hole, Murlog Patch, Among the Tits, Hossarse, Mud Hole, Coal Hole, Curlyweed, Off Grounds, Hills, Rough Ground, Viking Bank, Edge of Rough, Inner Hole, Dowsing Bank, and many, many more that were named after skippers who found the ground themselves and worked them year in, year out.

Once, when fishing in the trawler *River Spey*, we were hauling the starboard gear in. It was raining hard. I was wearing my oil frock and thinking that it was a good thing that I had oiled it with boiled linseed oil before that trip. I had taken it home and hung it up in the back yard to dry before taking it on board ship. The rain came down in buckets, and I didn't like it.

We had our fingers in the net, pulling it towards the shop's rail, untying the lazy decky and heaving on the cod ends to take the weight off the net. We could only see a few yards and it became very hot. The rain seemed to be very warm; the oil on my frock washed off and my shoulders were wet through.

I saw rain drops hitting the water and the splashes seemed six inches high. We could hardly see any distance at all. Then we heard a loud bang, the thunder seemed quite near to us. Then lightning seemed to strike the water very near to us indeed. My face was burning. I heard one of the crew say: 'We are in the centre of a storm.'

I did not frighten easily, but I, and the rest of the crew, thought we had had it. The faces of the crew on deck were an orange colour. Each time it thundered there was a cracking noise, and the lightning was very hot. We were about ten minutes in this storm before it moved away, northerly.

We got the cod ends aboard, no fish in them, only a hole at the bottom, telling us that we had picked up a large stone that had gone down the belly of the net, before tearing its way out again and taking the catch with it.

The third hand soon mended the hole. We shot the gear away and started to fish again. By this time the sky was clearing and, while I was taking my wet frock off, I saw a very unusual sight. I had never seen a water spout before, but about three to five miles away I saw this phenomenon. I told some of the crew to look at it. We thought the water was going upwards from the sea, but we were told later that it was a cloud burst and the water was actually coming down–though I'm not very sure that that was right.

I put my frock on a line that I had rigged up at the back of the funnel, just above the fidley grating (an escape hatch from the stoke hold). The heat from the furnace dried our wet clothing in a few minutes. After doing this it was my turn to have a sleep. Getting into my bunk, head down, I had soon forgotten all about the storm–or anything else.

Afterwards when gutting, or during meal times, I remember one of the crew saying: 'I wonder if any of our fishing boats that have been lost at sea, without any trace, in fine weather, have been sunk by one of these huge water spouts? There would be thousands of tons of water coming down on top of them.

BEFORE HOSTILITIES AND AFTER

Like many other Lincolnshire men, I started my fishing life in the North Sea. The old ships that I fished in were bug ridden and rat infested. Although stoved out now and again during a refit, within a few weeks the rats and bugs would be back again.

The vessels I sailed in were the Steam Trawlers *Balmoral, Carlton, Castleton. Cedric, Clacton, Coniston, Diamond, Emerald, Lacerta, Lacennia, Edwardian,* and *Prince Leo*, all Grimsby vessels, some of which were thirty years old.

The North Sea fishing grounds stretched one thousand miles long and approximately two hundred miles wide. Names such

136.

as these were fished quite regularly: Clay Deeps, Yorkshire Hole, Coal Hole, Bruce's Gardens, Tea Kettle Hole, Cleaver Bank, Viking Bank, Skaty, Mud Hole, Red House, The Hills, The Roughs, Silver Pit, Dogger, Curly, The Steps.

Trawling was a very hard life. Fishermen had to be strong; if one became ill there was no one to take his place. Each man had his own job; there were no spare hands allowed by the Board of Trade

The fishing grounds had their wrecks from the 1914 war. These were charted and we could keep away from them. Many skippers have been held fast by wrecks, tearing their nets to pieces, so the lead line was used very often to find the ship's position.

If we had a haul the skipper would look into the fish pound. Picking a bit of weed he would examine it closely and know how far the ship was from the River Humber, to a couple of miles or so. The sextant was used very rarely. The grounds, when fished properly, presented no problems and we could fish at one, five and nine, round the clock.

The firm's manager did not like to spend money on trawl gear. We had to make whatever we had aboard last. If we lost any net there was trouble in the office. The manager would have the skipper in his office and a big enquiry would take place. Sometimes a skipper would be replaced for losing some net. A net had to be proved to be really rotted before replacement. Net menders would come aboard in dock to replace rotten net: they were told to be sparing with new net and to mend the old if possible.

Sometimes, if we caught a bag of dogfish, the weight would pull the cod ends off the net, probably losing the lot. Fish caught in these grounds were good fish and we looked after it, and customers buying it on the pontoon were always saying how well it looked. We never made a fortune but we got a living. We were all happy-go-lucky.

Trawlers from different countries fished here. Seiners and

herring drifters in their hundreds dominated the grounds. We had to be very careful not to pick their nets up with the trawl. Large cargo boats steamed past, with timber cargoes and big yachts, with holiday people on board, would anchor in our fishing area at night. We fished around them, and we could often hear the music from their bands. During the day-time a small boat from one of these vessels would sometimes come alongside and they would ask for small fish for baiting their rods. Some of the yachting people were fishing for tunney fish, of which there was plenty in those days.

A few large whales would often swim near us, throwing their great tails into the air and make a loud noise as they hit the water.

When we were interrupted by the war, a lot of these old ships had to go. Many did not come back again–just like the fishermen.

The old fishermen's church in Grimsby has gone too. Many people went into the church to pray for their fishermen sons, or husbands, or boyfriends.

ICELAND

Iceland did not appeal to me at all. My best friend, lost with the Steam Trawler *Leicestershire* which sank in the Pentland Firth, made me feel sad about going there. And I was uncomfortable when I signed on the *S. T. Vizalma*, out of the Atlas firm managed by Letton's.

Standing on the corner near Dobby's outfitters, a skipper came to me and asked me if I would do a trip with him as mate because his own mate was sitting for his skipper's ticket and could not go for several weeks.

Being a bit short of money I decided to have a go. It was a bigger ship than I had fished in before, the fishroom seeming like a dance hall to me, and the ice we took looked smaller than usual because the fish pounds were so much larger than I had been used to seeing. Leaving the dock we soon passed

Flamborough Head. The crew sorted the bond out in their quarters and the watch was set. The skipper showed me the radar equipment and how it worked.

Steaming through the Pentland Firth in fine sunny weather it looked very nice, with the Orkneys standing out on the starboard side, and the coast of Scotland, with John o'Groats, on the port side looked lovely. We were soon on the last course to Iceland.

Going into the cabin I had a yarn with the cook, and the engineer who had just come off duty, neither of whom I had met before. It seemed a very strange world after the war. I believe out of the whole crew I had seen only one man before. To think that I had known hundreds of fishermen before the war, and now it seemed very different–quiet, very little talking to one another and not like it had been. I suppose it was just that we didn't know one another and each others families and friends. It used to be very happy-go-lucky, and that seemed very different.

Going on watch I was surprised to see that the little white speck I reported in the log book was the top of Mount Snowy in Iceland. I had seen it over one hundred miles away.

It had only taken seventy-two hours steaming from Spurn Light Vessel to the south shore of Iceland, where we started to fish. After towing the trawl for a couple of hours, the skipper decided to see if we had caught anything. To our surprise we had a net-full of large codlings. We had to make about ten lifts to bring them all aboard. No other ships were around and we shot the gear again hoping the fish were still there. During the fishing I saw a vessel aground on the low sands and asked the skipper its name. He told me it was the Steam Trawler *Grimsby Town*, which had run aground some time before and was a total loss.

We hauled again and had about the same catch as the first trawl. After a few days fishing, eighteen hours on six off, the skipper asked me how much fish we had down in the fish room.

As the ship was a lot bigger than I was used to I knew very little about how much the fish pounds held so the skipper came with me down to the fish room, and we had a reckon up. No fish pound had any fish above the stakeing. He said we had over two thousand kits aboard and now that the fish had taken off he was not prepared to steam around Iceland looking for more. We would go home, land what we had, and make a fresh start next trip.

Steaming home in fine weather, the crew were like a lot of cleaners at work, polishing the brasswork all over the ship; vents, port-hole covers, compass, anything that would shine had to be polished. The wheelhouse sides were polished with cod liver oil to make the woodwork shine. The third hand, with the help of a couple of men, stowed away the trawl nice and neatly. By the time we had entered the Pentland Firth the cleaning was almost done.

One of the crew, the one who was the only man I had known before the war, was given a bottle of rum. The skipper told him to drink some of it and then he would be allowed to take the bottle off the ship by the customs' officers. But once he had tasted the rum he drank the whole bottle. Lying on the deck, I saw him vomiting blood–the deck seemed to be awash with it. I told the skipper who contacted Aberdeen Hospital, saying we were bringing a man into port who was bleeding to death. This happened when we were about sixteen miles east of Aberdeen.

We were soon moored up and the police, about ten of them, were swarming on board looking for the chap who had stabbed him. The skipper, saying the crewman was bleeding badly, forgot to say that no one else was involved, so the police thought someone else had injured him.

After a few hours in Aberdeen Hospital, the crewman was out of danger, and he returned to Grimsby a few weeks later.

The two thousand kits of fish we landed on the eleventh day made two pounds a kit. I took two hundred pounds home for my share; we thought it was a lot of money then. The ship took nine days going from the Spurn Light Vessel to Iceland and back to the Spurn Light Vessel again. It was the shortest that I can remember going to Iceland and coming back with a trip.

After having a couple of days ashore, I was asked by the ship's runner if I would go for another trip in the *Vizalma* again, as the mate was still at the Nautical School, studying. Harold Moss, the runner for T.C. & F. Moss's firm, said that my own ship was still fitting out–so I signed on again.

Some of the crew had been replaced on this second voyage. I still did not know any of them. The weather got worse this trip, with very strong winds blowing. We had to shelter in Seydisfjordur fiords for two or three days. I believe we circumnavigated Iceland looking for fish. Steaming home after twenty-eight days at sea it was still rough and making the trawl fast to the ship's rail was quite a feat. Pulling on the ropes to tighten the net on the ship's side reminded me of a cowboy trying to ride a bucking horse at the rodeo, with the bows of the ship jumping into the air as each wave caught the starboard side of the buff.

Coming into the Pentland Firth it calmed down, and passing Duncansby Head, we got down to cleaning and stowing again.

The trip and bad weather forgotten, I signed off, and went back to fishing in the North Sea.

CHAPTER 11

S. T. LACENNIA AND THE ROSE OF ENGLAND, 1948

W. W. BUTT'S FIRM WAS IN AUCKLAND ROAD, FISHDOCKS, GRIMSBY. I was talking outside their offices to several fishermen who had come back home from the Royal Navy, when I was approached by Jack Rouse, the ship's runner for W. W. Butts,, outside his office. He asked me if I would go as mate of the Steam Trawler *Lacennia*, fishing the White Sea. I did not know any of these men. Some were Scotsmen and there were six others from various ports who had come to Grimsby looking for a boat to fish on; and Jack Rouse gave them one.

The skipper was only a young chap; I had never seen him before either. He told me what he wanted and how he wanted things running, and then we left the dock. The log set, we steamed for the Norwegian coast. Once on a course, we set the watch, twelve crew again, no extra hands.

We steamed a long while before we sighted Bear Island in the distance. The skipper took his position and we stood by to shoot the trawl as soon as he was ready. We had been very busy while steaming in the fine weather, putting a new trawl alongside, and making sure that the fishroom was ready for the catch, if any.

Suddenly we heard the ring of the telegraph, the engines stopped, and the skipper shouted to get the trawl over the side. The crew were very good fishermen, wherever they may have come from. I hardly had to speak to them at all, everything was done like clockwork

We had a meal whilst the trawl was being towed, the skipper saying that it would be a short tow to see if any fish were about. After about one and a half hours we hauled and found that we had to make fifteen bags to get all the fish on deck–mostly cod. We thought this was our lucky break, but it was not to be.

We shot away, time and time again, towing for an hour at a time, but not one fish did we catch again at Bear Island. So we steamed to the White Sea grounds, with the skipper blaming everything there was for his bad luck. The cod ends had to be tied up either by me or another man, the skipper saying that the third hand, whose job it should have been, was unlucky. He screamed his head off at times which upset the crew. Eventually, after a few days' steaming, we saw smoke from several vessels, Russian and Hull trawlers, fishing together two hundred miles north of Cape Kanin, off the Russian coast. The cod we had caught off Bear Island I iced again and covered with several layers of pound boards. We had to keep the air out, knowing it would be many days old by the time it was landed, and it was summer time, too. I had to be careful not to land rotten fish; we had no freezers then.

We shot away the trawl among the Russian vessels and hauled the gear every two hours, catching some nice fish; cod, haddocks, one or two halibut. The third hand gutted the halibut.

Hauling the trawl up one day, we heard a loud crack. We had to heave very carefully because the plate on the starboard side piston on the winch had cracked in half. The chief engineer was asked to look at this, and repair it if he could. He told us he had a spare piston rod and plate fastened to the bulwarks in the engine room. So after all the fish had been gutted and iced down in the fishroom, the crew gave a hand to manhandle this heavy machinery onto the deck. It needed a very large spanner to take the iron nuts off, but the engineer did not have one aboard. As the nearest port was Vardo, on the north east coast of Norway, about two hundred and fifty miles away, the skipper decided to go there and have the broken part taken off. I can remember him and the chief engineer going ashore, at this small port, to find a fitter. Very few people came near us. I spoke to a young fisherman who had come here from Canada when he was a baby; He caught grundibo for a living From his boat he would hook these large mammals, bringing them to the top of the water; he then slit those that were too heavy to lift on board, and then let the fish, or mammal, go back into the sea. Doing this for three months of the year kept him, his mate, and the boat for the rest of the year. The skipper came back with a very old man and a boy of about fourteen years of age, to have a look at the size of the nut which had to come off. The old chap said he would make a spanner for the engineer, and would be back in a day or so.

I enquired if there was a hospital near by. Looking at Vardo when we entered, it looked like an island to me. One of the fishermen told me the hospital was not far away, and directed me. The following day, after the work was done on deck, I put my ration of bonded tobacco, cigarettes and other items in a parcel to give to anyone wanting a smoke at the hospital. Very few ships visited Vardo, and tobacco was a luxury in those days.

Walking towards some small wooden huts someone told me that they were the hospital. A young nurse, who could speak a little broken English, told me with a smile that only two Norwegians were patients at the hospital just now. However, as I was giving the parcel to her, she told me they had two Englishmen in the wards, who had been there many months, and they classed them as Norwegian now. One fisherman was from Hull, the other from Grimsby. After visiting the Yorky and shaking hands with him I went to see the Grimsby chap who knew me straight away but I did not recognise him; the poor chap was very thin and looked as if he had been in great pain for a long time. He told me a remarkable story, how the vessel he had been in, the Grimsby Steam Trawler *Vilda*, had been dodging about during a bad gale in the Barents Sea. She had been laid to for some time and at meal times, the food on the cabin table kept sliding from one side to the other, sometimes even going into the bunks, so the skipper rang the telegraph for slow speed ahead, to try to stop the rolling. After the meal the crew, coming out of the foc'sle, had to wait for a chance to run aft, taking a hold on the life line which was rigged up from forward to the winch barrel.

'Going aft, a large wave came inboard and took me overboard with it,' he told me. 'Another wave swept me back onboard, smashing my body on the bridge side. Then another wave coming at almost the same time swept me over the side again. The vessel, on its beam ends, had the after mast near the water, and another wave hooked me onto the after mizzen boom. The ship was now heading into the wind very slowly, dipping her bows up and down, which made it possible for a young Scotsman deckhand to get me down.'

'I was brought into Vardo eleven months ago, with seventeen fractures.'

The nurses had looked after him very well. I noticed a small window above his pillow. He told me an old lady who sometimes visited him gave him a looking glass so he could see out of the window. She gave him a bible. He told me a donkey looked in at him sometimes, poking its head though the window frame.

He asked me to let his parents know he would be home in about three months' time. Talking to him about his family I found out who he was without him realising that I hadn't recognised him as he was, lying in bed looking very ill. When I returned home I told his father that he would be coming home shortly, which he did. The same nurse from Vardo looked after him in the old Grimsby hospital for six weeks.

He still lives in Grimsby, with his old dog, and has pains from that accident even now.

On the third day in Vardo, the old man and the lad came back, with this large, very heavy, own-made spanner,. After some hours, when the job was done and tested, we left Vardo for the fishing grounds again. The skipper was on the bottle, shouting and screaming, but the crew took very little notice of him, just swearing at him if he came near to them.

We were fishing very near the coast. Several small Russian fishing vessels were near us. We had a dan buoy down to keep us on the fishing ground, towing one hour away from it and them returning to it. Then a Russian fishing boat picked it up, and we didn't see it again. Our skipper, full of drink, wanted to chase after this boat, but we reasoned with him, saying that it would get us into trouble.

So he decided to call it a day and we steamed for home. We had been at sea nearly a month. At the lock pits I reported the amount of fish we had caught but, coming down at 4.00 a.m., I was surprised to see all the fish out on the pontoon. The halibuts we had caught numbered forty on my tally and each one had been looked after and iced on its own. On the pontoon I counted eleven.

I had heard of the 'Ghost Train', but this was the first time I had experienced this sort of thing. There were almost two hundred kits short of my fish tally, too.

I wanted to make a report about this to the Board of Trade, but, as I was in the RNR, I had to report to *HMS Victory* (Portsmouth Barracks) to do an exercise with the Royal Navy. When I returned the incident was forgotten.

THE GREAT NORTH POND

The docks seemed always to be full of ships before the war; seiners, from every port in Denmark and Sweden; herring drifters, Scotch, English, and Dutch; trawlers from France, Germany, Holland and other ports; many were the larger trawlers being built for distant fishing grounds. You did not have to walk round the dock to reach the other side, you could go across the ships moored together. Any vessel could be watered wherever it was moored since the water hydrants were close together from the lock pit to the lock pit round the docks.

146.

Coal was loaded under the hoists on the east side; three hoists, with six large buckets, were lowered with tons of coal throughout the twenty four hours of the day and night. The coal was delivered by hundreds of wagons each day, they waited in the sidings at Clee Station until they were shunted to the hoists.

Ice was made in blocks by The Grimsby Ice Company on the docks, and it was crushed as it was sent round the ice shutes, along the south and west quays: there were usually many ships all being iced at the same time. Many tugs shuttled the trawlers to these places. Ice was also made in Victor Street at the Ice House. Horses and carts took barrels of ice from there to the docks. Another Ice House was in East March Street and from here chain driven vehicles went to and fro with ice packed very tightly in bags, to the docks.

Food was barrowed to the ships and put aboard by the watchman. For many years Mr. Ward took the fishermen's clothing from Dobby's, Colebrook's, or Red House Stores, on a horse and cart, for a few pence each.

* * * * *

Fishing the turbot bank, in nice weather, with a westerly breeze, we would catch eight to ten baskets of turbot a haul. When we had a good haul, we dropped a dan buoy in the vicinity and trawled around it, until the fishing slacked off and we moved off again, picking the dan buoy up as we sailed to another position. On finding more fish, we would drop the dan buoy again.

The only trouble we had was that we could never discover where the fish went to when the wind changed to easterly. We would be catching fish, wind very light, westerly; change of wind, still very light, but now easterly–but now no fish, or maybe a large but very thin turbot, or one with sores on its body. Change of wind again, and the fish were back once more.

147.

The skipper said no-one seemed to know where they went to, when the wind changes to the east. This happened all the time that I was fishing the Pond.

A school of horse mackerel might come swimming by in their thousands past the ship, making a ripple on the water that was two hundred yards long and fifty yards wide. I wondered how deep the shoal was. On one occasion another trawler came alongside to ask if we were catching much, its skipper speaking through his voice trumpet. Our skipper asked if we could find his trumpet so that he could reply. It was eventually found, after a lot of searching.

I Remember Wives at Sea–Before the War

A few Grimsby skippers took their wives to sea with them, for a trip to Iceland or the White Sea, during the summer months.

No cameras were allowed on foreign going vessels in those days, so not many pictures were taken at sea with them on board. In those days the Russians would have put us in jail for having a camera, thinking that we were spying on them. I remember one incident when a Grimsby trawler was boarded by a Russian submarine crew who had the idea that the skipper's wife was a spy and they escorted the vessel into a Russian port. The skipper's wife tried to explain that she had a family of children in Grimsby and wanted to go home. She was in custody for a few weeks, until the authorities sorted her story out. Eventually she was allowed to go free.

Another Grimsby skipper's wife was on board a Grimsby vessel in Norway. Calling at Tromsö for ice and stores, she wanted to have a look around the town. She had forgotten to take a blouse with her, and the cook had to make her one out of a flour bag he had boiled. The flour came aboard in those days in one hundredweight bags made of white cotton.

I remember one woman going to sea that many times she steamed the ship whilst fishing so that her husband could have a sleep, waking him up at hauling time.

During my fishing life, the most interesting vessel that I worked on, was the old *Rose of England*. Built in Liverpool in 1909, she had fifty-two years of sea life.

I would not be telling the truth if I said it was the best sea ship I had sailed on, or the cleanest. During heavy weather the water came over the starboard and portside quarters, filling up to the rail top. If you did not know her, you would have water up to your waistline, going to the galley every two or three minutes. She was a dirty so-and-so.

The rats didn't like to leave either. We had a rat hunt every now and again during fine weather whilst towing the trawl. We would ask the engineer to start the donkey pump, then take away all movable items from the deck under the whale back. The pressure from the hose pipe washed the rats from their hiding places. They lived and bred in the wings on each side of the ship, where the spare coal for emergencies was carried, and of course it was very seldom needed so they would usually be undisturbed.

The rats made their nests there, bringing the young on deck at night. We washed dozens overboard, and they were soon swallowed up by the big black and white seagulls. If we left any fish in baskets, at night you could see rats carrying even very large fish forward in their mouths. We saw the bones when washing down.

Alf Redvers Walker was the skipper; he had been skipper for many years on the Grimsby trawler *Drummer Boy*. Changing over to the *Rose*, he became one of the North Pond's biggest money earners. During the war, he made many good fishing trips.

I signed on as mate with Alf and we worked together, making it easy to keep a good crew; there was no screaming and shouting, everything went like clockwork. We would work the Silver Pits trying to find a few soles. We'd leave the south side in eighteen fathoms, towing north, and then drop straight down into thirty-two fathoms, having to let more warp out in the deeper water. If we tried to tow back again onto the eighteen fathoms, it was hard lines. We would hit a large wall of stones, like hitting a brick wall, that stopped the ship in its wake. We would haul the net, only to find that we had a nice bag of stones for the rockery, or a hole in the cod ends where the stones had gone through.

If we had carried on towing across the mile wide gap of the Silver Pit, we would have gradually come out of thirty-five fathoms to shoal in seven, but we should have had to stop a long time before we towed that shallow. Our trawl would have been full of curly brown weed, which grows to a great height. If we did happen to get away with a tow in this weed, we would have caught the finest plaice that exist on the Dogger Bank: big brown-skinned plaice with large, bright red spots on them one inch thick, some weighing six, seven, or even eight pounds. But nine times out of ten we would come fast, and have only a huge bag of weed to shovel back over the side again, with maybe just one or two nice plaice.

During very bad northerly gales wreckage can be seen on the top of the Dogger Bank. Many ships have been lost there. Fishing on the Dogger Bank in late summer time when it's very hot, makes the crew's hands and faces itch, and sores appear, bluish in colour. Some crews are very allergic to the steam that rises from the curly weed and boils in dozens appear on arms and neck. Some men have refused to work on the bank because of this, knowing they would then have to remain ashore for many weeks, recovering.

In the winter months, fishing on the south side of the pits, and keeping in thirty-two fathoms, we used to catch sixteen to twenty baskets of nice large plaice.

It was about this time of year when we picked up a bottle in the trawl. After the crew had washed the fish, the hose was played on the bottle to clean the mud and dirt from it. A small tree was growing from the cork, and barnacles with coral covered the glass. Giving the small tree a good wash, it turned out to be whelk spawn, a good twelve inches high, growing on the cork. It was a very bright yellow colour.

Looking into the light between the coral and barnacles, I saw the letter B and an L followed by a Y. I presumed this was an old Bellamy's bottle. Taking care of it, I took it home.

Word soon got around about the bottle. There was more fuss about it than if we had found ten mines. A knock came on my door after I had only been in dock a few hours–Ronald C. Bellamy.

'I have come to see the bottle which was picked up by your vessel during your last fishing voyage,' he said.

I showed it to him. He examined it for a few minutes, saying, 'Yes it is one of mine. I would like to have it for my son.'

I told him it belonged to him and he could keep it. He was pleased and gave my boy a treat for it. Mr. R. C. Bellamy was High Sheriff of Lincolnshire.

The large oysters we caught in the trawl were quickly eaten by the skipper, who loved to open them and swallow them at once. Crabs, prawns, and queens, were always looked after by our cook, Mr. Pike, and cleaned and bottled to be shared later with the crew during our waiting time in the river.

Towing one day during early morning, the light just showing, I saw a mine floating ahead of me, with its large horns showing. Too late to call hands on deck, I just moved the wheel very lightly to port, hoping the mine would clear the warps, aft. Just as it came into the wash of the bows, it moved a few feet to starboard. I gave a sigh of relief as we passed it. Looking at it astern, I saw, written in large white letters on it: 'DUMMY'.

I often think to myself, if we had hit it, would it have been a dummy?

New ships were beginning to arrive in Grimsby, bound for Icelandic fishing grounds, the Norwegian coast, Bear Island and the White Sea. More crews were needed to man them as the Board of Trade allowed twice as many men go to sea on one of these larger vessels. One vessel fished from the stern, which was a new idea. All the ships I had sailed on were side winders. My old mates who had come back from the war went fishing in these larger ships. I had an occasional trip in one, but I stuck to the North Pond. Of the best fishermen in the new ships, many were lost in the fiords, and the bad weather took its toll. The skippers believed the ships could stand anything the gods sent, including gales.

The crew of the *Rose* consisted of skipper, mate, third hand, two engineers, two deck hands, one cook, one trimmer. We all lived within a mile of each other. Old Ben Germany was the chief engineer, Alf Walker skipper, Joe Tideswell third hand, the deck hand was Fred, and the trimmer was Harry. The others I cannot remember, but I know Bing Beals, the entertainer, came on several trips, and who still goes in the clubs singing 'Mule Train'. Duggy Knight was another deck hand.

While we gutted in the fish pounds, Fred would often have a fit. He suffered from epilepsy. The poor chap had to earn a living so we took him with us, deck hands were scarce then, and I looked after him when he was in a fit. He did his work O.K. and he never complained, no matter how hard the job he was doing. Anyway we all liked him. When he had a fit, we would drag him behind the winch, let Alf, the skipper, know, and he would look after Fred until he came round again.

Some time during my fishing days all trawlers were fitted with a walkie talkie telephone, to call one another up. It was like hell on earth with them all trying to speak at the same time. The *Rose of England's* skipper would call his pal up on the *Magnolia*, at the same time someone else would be calling us. It just did not work, not until a roster was made out in the office for skippers to speak to each other at given times only.

If you happened to be on a bit of fish with a buoy down marking the spot, you talked to your mate on the phone to come to you, and in half an hour you would have twenty ships fishing around your buoy, sweeping all the fish up. So a code was used. Still the other ships guessed, and usually there was soon more company than was wanted.

So, later on, the talkie telephone was used very little. Calling the wife was one idea that Alf had. She could pick him up on the old wireless set she had. He spoke over the air at 11.00 p.m. and she could hear him speaking; she'd then send him a message back by her phone to the office if required. She could not speak to him then, but in later years she could telephone to Humber Radio and speak to the ship from her home via them.

Now you can telephone anywhere you like, from sea to shore, or vice versa.

The fish we landed was sold by Sam and George Bee, great fish dock characters and, I reckon, the best fish salesmen. They always said: 'Vic, you look after the fish, and we will sell it for you.' I always had good fish, and looked after it well. Old Harry Stratton, the trimmer, chopping the ice for me, knew to a shovelfull how much the fish required.

Young Stan Marshall was a learner salesman for us, under the G.B.'s wing, selling the rough fish we caught–gurnard, dogs, cats, and so on. Now he is a fish salesman himself, on Grimsby pontoon every morning, shouting his head off, 'Cod . . . cod . . . cod here', or 'Plaice . . . plaice . . . plaice here'. It's nice to hear his voice in the early morning; wakes all the buyers up, and me too, at times.

When we caught a large sturgeon Stan sold it to Mudds' firm, who had it delivered to Buckingham Palace. At the same time we also caught a small sturgeon, which we cut up, and the cook prepared it for us. I do not know how he cooked it, boiled or roasted, all I know is it tasted very woody. None of the crew ate it. throwing most of it overboard.

After landing our fish, the board washer would scrub our pound boards one by one and stack them on the deck. We, the crew, would put them all in the fish room, stacked neatly in each pound, ready to bring out, when we put the fish away again.

In August 1952, a north-east gale was blowing in the North Sea. It was one of those nasty come-quickly winds which abated after twenty-four hours, but with the wind being north-east the swell was very bad, and lasted for days.

We were near the end of our trip, having been at sea for ten days. Alf said it was no good laying and dodging, it was too late in the trip, we would go home to Grimsby and land the fish. We had been fishing sixty miles north-east of the river.

Arriving in the early morning, the fish dock gates were open, so we moored very near to Scrobs Corner, near the west lock pits (not in use now). After landing our fish, some of the crew went home. I was putting the fish-room pound boards down the hatch and the skipper was about to shut the wireless telephone off when he heard the skipper of the Steam Trawler *Magnolia* calling the *Rose of England* to come in

Alf Walker, our skipper, talked for about five minutes to Snowy Wing, the skipper of the *Magnolia*. He told Alf that his ship was taking a lot of water in and needed assistance. A pump would help, he said. Alf got on to our office, who delivered a pump for us to take out to the *S.T. Magnolia*, it being from the same firm as us (Franklins).

I was ready to go ashore, having had no sleep for many hours. The cook, one engineer and one deck hand had already gone home, leaving the skipper, myself, third hand, one decky, one trimmer, one engineer. Snowy was a very good friend of Alf's, and rather than ask another vessel, he wanted his friend to help him.

I told Alf to ask Snowy if any other vessel was near him, so that it could stand by until we arrived. He said that another vessel had been to him but it had now left. His position was somewhere in the region of forty-five miles north-east of the Spurn Light Vessel.

I didn't like it a bit. We were all tired and had had no food, no tea, no coffee, the cook having cleared everything out for a new lot to come on board. Leaving the river, we began to meet the swell, and the waves were coming over the whaleback. 'Good thing I had battened everything down,' I thought.

With only one engineer, I reckon we were doing ten knots, which meant one hour up the river, and four hours to the *Magnolia's* position. We should be able to see him about 2.00 p.m. Passing the first shipping lane seemed to take a long time, but we eventually got to the second shipping lane, keeping a good look out.

At last we saw the *Magnolia*, wallowing about in the water. I had a long line attached to the pump, with a small extra can of petrol tied to it. Getting as near to the *Magnolia* as he dared, the skipper asked me to throw the line, which was soon grabbed by my school pal Joe Grant, who was third hand of the *Magnolia*. The pump was soon started.

Snowy asked Alf if he would tow him towards the river while they pumped out. The wind had abated but the swell was north-east, and still running badly. I climbed on the whaleback, taking a long heaving line with me, which I intended to throw aboard the *Magnolia*. Our skipper asked me to use our warps for the tow, as they were thicker and stronger than Snowy's, he said. I agreed with him. We had some second-hand warps from one of our Iceland vessels, twice the size we normally used.

While we were trying to take a position to pass the warps aboard, our two bows were only a few feet away from one another, bobbing up and down in the swell together. I saw a young deck hand, Roland Willis, climb on to the whale back of the *Magnolia*. While I was speaking to him he threw me a parcel in a cloth, some tea, milk and sugar. The skipper must have asked Snowy for some when on the phone, as we had not had a drink since leaving the dock. I said to the deck hand: 'While we are bobbing about like this, jump on board of us. You cannot do anything on your ship.' But it was too late, by the time he made his mind up, the two vessels were further apart.

Making a small bladder fast to the heaving line, I was going to let the bladder blow on the water to the *Magnolia*, so that their crew could pull our warps on board. But Joe Tikeswell, our third hand, had not been idle. Waiting for an opportunity, he had thrown a heaving line aboard the *Magnolia*, making the two warps fast on their forward bollards and I had tightened the brakes on the winch, which had the whole weight, with two warps now towing the *Magnolia*. I let about three ships' length of warp out, took some turns on the after bits, and we started the tow.

Very steadily we turned before the swell. Looking at the *Magnolia* being towed, I did not feel happy. Why had the skipper waited so long for us to come all this way when other vessels were in the vicinity? I could see fishing vessels abut five miles away from him. Anyway, the swell was a nuisance and very soon washed the pump overboard.

I went on the bridge to steer while the skipper spoke on the wireless telephone to the *Magnolia*. During the tow I asked the trimmer to find the best axe he could, in case we needed it, and put it near the bollards. We had Freddy on board, and I hoped he didn't go into one of his epileptic fits whilst we were doing this towing job.

Keeping my eyes on the compass, I had the wheelhouse door fastened back in the open position, so I could turn and look at the tow every few minutes. I asked the skiper to speak to Snowy on the phone and ask him to wave or show a flag if he needed to speak to us on deck.

I could not see any of our crew, and very little of the *Magnolia's* crew either. Our crew could have been in the galley. Alf was down in his cabin sitting near the telephone, the cabin being underneath the wheelhouse. The skipper's cabin on the *Magnolia* was in the same place, but the entrance was in a different position, at the back part of the wheelhouse, where it was more awkward to climb up and down the steps. From where I was standing and steering the *Rose of England* I could see down into the skipper's berth and if I needed him, I could shout to him.

While in the wheelhouse, looking through the starboard side window which I had opened to its fullest position, I could see several stacks smoking to the westward of us. I presumed these were in the outer big boat track. It seemed hours before we passed them, with about thirty miles still to go, I reckoned.

Looking back at my tow, an uneasy feeling came over me. Were the bows of my tow getting higher every time I looked back at her? The swell seemed to come over the *Magnolia's* stern more easily, right along her decks. I did not feel satisfied with my tow at all.

Shouting down the hoodway, I spoke to our skipper, to ask Snowy to come off the *Magnolia* with his crew now. I could see no reason why they should be on board doing nothing, their vessel was now lying lower by the stern and it was worrying me.

Alf, picked the phone up and called the *Magnolia*, the approximate time was 4.00 p.m. He told Snowy what I had asked, telling him I thought the ship was in danger of capsizing, the bows being higher than when I looked half an hour ago. Snowy Wing replied that he would look down the cabin to see if she was taking any more water in, and would report back. He seemed to be a long time coming back, maybe fifteen minutes. I heard him on the phone, telling Alf that he believed no more water was going into the cabin and could we take him and his crew off the *Magnolia* at 8.30 p.m., at dusk, before darkness fell.

I felt very disappointed and told Alf not to speak on the phone to him any more, and make conversation on deck, as it would be awkward for Snowy to climb the steps going to and from his cabin. But Snowy thought his ship was O.K. and would make it home.

The smoke from our stack was belching black, blowing over our bows very slowly now the wind had dropped, but the swell still lingered on. About nineteen and a half miles to the river now. As I turned to look at my tow again, like a horse standing up on its hind legs, the bows rose up in the air. At the same time I could hear the *Magnolia's* skipper shouting through the

157.

phone, 'Alf, she's going, she's turning over.' In ten seconds it was all over, she had gone.

We were stunned.

I ran to the winch and opened the brakes to save us from being dragged down with her. The warps were screaming as they came off the drums.

The skipper, now on the bridge, told me the *Magnolia's* crew were swimming in the sea. I said if he put a strain on the warps I could chop through them and try to pick up the survivors. One axe was all I had to chop through these heavy warps. The ship's weight was tight to the *Magnolia* as I swung the axe, sparks flying each time a strand of wire snapped. Eventually they parted: we were free. How long it took I will never know.

'If those warps had caught your legs they would have chopped them off,' said Joe Tideswell, standing near me looking dazed. Joe was our third hand, a very nice, quiet chap, knew his job inside out.

I said, 'Joe, we have a lot of work to do. Men are left in the sea.' It was impossible for us to launch the lifeboat; anyway it had not been in the water for many years.

'I will go in the whaleback. Pass me as many lifebelts as we have on board, with long lines attached to each one. I'll guide the skipper to each man in the water and when I throw the lifebelt, you and Harry, and Freddy as well, can pull them in until I climb down and help you to pull them inboard. And if Freddy has a fit, throw him over as well!'

Freddy looked at me and said he would try his best. I felt a bit sorry for Joe, but what could we do? Giving him the end of number one lifebelt I saw a man in the water just keeping afloat, the mate from the *Magnolia*. I directed the skipper to him, threw the lifebelt and it landed alongside him and was soon grabbed. Joe and the crew pulled him in and aboard. The *Magnolias* cook had one leg shorter than the other. One boot he wore was about six or eight inches thick, and hollow, it helped to keep him afloat. I threw the lifebelt to him and he was soon aboard.

158.

Looking for the others, I saw that they seemed to have drifted quite a long way apart. I had to keep on the whaleback to show Alf where they were. I believe the next lad we picked up lived at the mission in Riby Square. Alf turned the ship round towards him, and I threw him a lifebelt. The vessel was bouncing in the swell, when the lifebelt hit him on the head and down he went. Shouting to Joe that I should have to jump in the sea for him and that he would have to pull both of us in together. As I was about to jump overboard I was surprised to see him come up, straight into the lifebelt and put both arms across the sides. I gave a sigh of relief as the crew pulled him on board.

The engineer and trimmer were next to come aboard, leaving Joe Grant, the third hand, still in the water, a long way from us. All the lifebelts were in a tangle on the deck. I could see Joe Tideswell had lost his trousers and Freddy and Harry stood like statues, wondering if they were dreaming this lot.

As I guided the *Rose* to my old shipmate and friend, who was floundering about barely conscious, we shouted to him to hang on, we were going to get him somehow. To keep him awake we kept shouting to him. Having no lifebelt, I climbed to the galley top where we kept a very old life-raft made of wood with an iron tank inside and hand lifelines fastened round it. Seeing Joe Grant about fifteen yards off our port quarter, I lifted this heavy life-raft above my head. When the vessel rolled to port I threw it about two feet short of Joe, who by this time was nearly unconscious. We were all screaming at him to hold onto the raft, which was now quite near him. He laid over the raft while we threw heaving lines on top of him, and gently pulled him and the raft inboard.

We got Joe into our cabin. I cut his clothes off with my knife, and we rubbed him down with towels, and laid him in my bunk.

Going on deck I heard skipper Walker saying that the engineer off the *Magnolia* was dead. He had hit his head on the rollers when jumping overboard from the sinking ship. We laid him forward on some blankets.

Three men died: Skipper Snowy Wing, Albert Foster (engineman) and Roland Willis (deckhand).

Steaming towards the river, someone made a jug of tea. Alf Walker poured a bottle of Compo in it, Compo being a medicine he had for coughs and colds. It was hot, like pepper. I gave all the crew a cup of this apiece, and the survivors were walking around very shortly after drinking it. Coming into the river, we had the flag at half mast.

The port's mission had to carry out the sad work just as they have done for many years, informing relatives of the lost and dead. Many people thought the two ships were at anchor in the river. Someone in authority had informed the *Grimsby Evening Telegraph* that the *Rose of England* had towed the *Magnolia* to the anchorage at the Burcombe light vessel. Some of the *Magnolia's* crew's relatives were expecting their sons and husbands to walk into the house at any moment. Instead it was the Mission Officer with his sad story.

Our crew deserved a medal of distinction for what they did that day. No drink or food on board, just took it as an ordinary day's work. Not one of the crew was thanked by anyone for what they did. If the ship had been saved I believe it would have been a different tale.

Many years later I sat in a hotel at Louth, in Lincolnshire. While my wife and I were in the lounge, a man and woman sat oposite to us. The man kept looking at me and rubbing his head. This went on for some time until he asked me if I knew him. When I replied that I didn't, he told me that he was the man I had hit on the head with the lifebelt. He had not gone back to sea any more.

George Horner, the mate of the *Magnolia*, I saw once in the country. Joe Grant, third hand, sailed with me later, and is now watching on the docks. Joe Tideswell lives in the country, I have seen him only once in many years. Freddy and Harry I have not seen. Alf died a few years later.

After the sad bereavements I could see that Alf Walker had

taken it very hard. People were saying we should not have gone out that morning, we should have let a vessel nearer to them look into it. I only wished Alf had switched the telephone off when we came into dock. We would not have heard anything and we would have gone home.

But when a pal was in need, what would they have done?

Not long after we slipped out of the dock one morning, early, to start fishing about sixty miles north-east of the river. Setting the log at the Spurn Light Vessel on a nice calm day, I took the wheel to steer along. Alf, in his working gear, came on the deck with hammer and nails, asking the new deck hand to bring him some pound boards. I wondered what he was doing, he had not said anything to me. Looking out of the wheelhouse window I saw him making a raft. Later he brought three or four wreaths from his berth, which must have been delivered whilst we were at home.

He made them fast to the raft, and came back on the bridge asking me to leave him alone while he tried to find the spot where the *Magnolia* had gone down, with Snowy and Roland Willis still on board. After the log showed nineteen and a half miles north-east of the river, I said that we could not be far from it now. Having one of the first Decca machines on board, Alf stopped the engines. I sat on the starboard rail looking into the water. I told one of the crew: 'Look down here'. I could see the bladder I had tied on the long heaving line, which young Willis was going to use for our warps.

The end of the line must have been tied to the windlass on the bows. When going down the bladder would rise to the surface, because of the tide flowing. It was now just below the surface. I couldn't believe it.

We let the raft float above the *Magnolia* and stood silent for some time. Alf moved away from us and went down to his berth crying. Taking the wheel again, we carried on to the fishing grounds.

As I mentioned before, the crews were now a problem. New

ships were coming to Hull, Grimsby, and Fleetwood; and the crews coming aboard us who were well-trained soon left for the bigger ships and the bigger money.

Some of the older men, Bill Redgrift, Harry Stratton, Meadows, old Tally Fish, Campaign Smithy, Military George, were all getting on in life. They had signed on these vessels 'at the age of sixty' for the previous ten years. Some of them had passed seventy and were still going to sea, until one ship went into Denmark for repairs. A photographer, taking photos of old Grimsby fishermen, accidentally told their ages; and the crafty old devils were stopped from signing on ships again.

You could call at any local and see at least four of these old fishermen, playing fives and threes for a copper or two, hoping for a young fisherman to come in the bar and pay for a drink all round–which was done quite often. Going to pay for a drink, you would be surprised to hear the barmaid say that your drink had been paid for, but whoever had left the money had gone on to another pub.

We had a new third hand. He told me he had four children to his wife, and another four to his concubine who lived in the same house. He said that both the women, and all the eight children, loved him and that they all lived happily together!

CHAPTER 12

THE HALCYON DAYS–AND AFTER

THERE WAS PEACE AND HAPPINESS FOR ALL in those halcyon pre-war days. One hundred and ten pubs to visit; not very much money about, but ships landing every day bar Sunday, and luggers bringing fresh herrings early every morning into the Royal Dock Basin. Trawlers landing in dozens and everyone was working: the dry docks were full of trawlers and the slipways full of ships. You could hear the riveters hammering away. Our ship was having a fit out, and my wife was drawing £5 per week pay, which I should have to pay back out of my settlings when we started fishing again. The government paid a small grant to each vessel if they did not make enough money to pay the expenses. After the war it was not the same.

* * * * * *

The Mission was always open in the early hours, with many old fishermen sitting on the plush seats around the rooms having a cuppa. It was nice to have them greet you with a nod or a doff of their caps. They were all respectable and respected and all were nice and clean. Sometimes they had a treat if the younger fishermen came in for a drink of tea or coffee. They would be off like lightning to the 'Lord Ragland' at 11.00 a.m. if they had got a hedger-in (slang for enough money for half a pint). The Lord Ragland was a small pub opposite to the Mission; it was knocked down many years ago.

Fishing again after fitting out, the third hand was asked to put some new cod ends on the trawl. These cod ends had never been used by any ship until Alf Walker, while he was at home, asked Mr. Franklin if he could have some stronger ones made

163.

up. We had been picking something heavy up on our fishing gound and it was going straight through the meshes of our twine cod ends, so he would like some nylon ones made. Where the firm bought this line from I don't know, but it would have held a railway train in. It was thick, green, and made a flat net. The third hand had false bellies and one half of a cowhide, so we fixed them on the net. Shooting the trawl, we towed in No Man's Land again, where we had always previously had the cod ends torn out.

The engineer told the skipper the ship was slowing down so would we haul, as we might have picked up something heavy. Heaving the gear up very slowly, the tackle in the becket, we hauled the cod ends over the rail inboard, to see another mine in the net. Lowering it slowly onto the deck, the third hand untied the knot while I stood by watching, heaving the net off and leaving the mine and fish in the pound.

All at once a hissing sound came from the mine. Looking round, I was going to ask what they believed was causing this noise, but I was on my own. The crew had fled aft. Moving some fish and dirt from the mine I found it had a rifle bullet hole in it and air was coming from it. We tied it up forward on some net, to dump later.

It was now winter: the *Magnolia* incident was over and no longer talked about.

I was on the bridge steering while towing, my watch mate making the tea for the 5.00 a.m. hauling time; the engineer was in the galley with him, waiting for the tea to mash. He would take a cup of tea down the engine room with him, and my watch mate would bring me one, then he would clean the galley fire and tidy up ready for the cook coming on duty.

I could hear the forestays and halliards tapping on the mast, a small sharp whistling sound. 'Hello, the wind is getting up', I thought. A small spray started to blow over the starboard bow, the ship began to roll more frequently. It was a good thing we were all electric; now the lights on the mast could be seen for miles, the port and starboard lights were very clear. Even the after stern light fixed on the mast aft could be seen for more than two miles.

It was still dark. I put all the deck lights on just by pulling a switch. It was like Blackpool lit up, compared with the old gas and oil lamps we used to have. Ten minutes to hauling time, my mate called: 'All hands out from foreward'. The third hand slept aft, he was called out too. I went down to the skipper's berth calling him by name. You never, never touched a man to wake him up, not fishing anyhow, it was not done. Coming up onto the bridge I went to the steam winch to run it ready for my watch to knock out, heaving the gear up after the warps had been knocked out of the block.

The two otter doors came up first. It was the duty of the trimmer to bring the forward quarter rope to the winch. The after quarter rope was brought to the winch by the deck hand. Heaving these two ropes together brought the bobbins to the topside rail, when the third hand put a slip hook in the quarter shackle. When the fore end showed, the jilson hook was put in the fore quarter shackle and heaved up. When the bobbins were inboard, the shout of 'Let go!' was heard, and the bobbins with everything else dropped on the deck. The headline was grabbed very quickly and the net pulled inboard by all hands, the skipper giving us a hand if needed. The third hand's job was to put a becket round his cod ends and heave them aboard, letting go of the codline he had tied up with a very special knot.

With the fish on deck, the cod ends were quickly inspected for any holes or damage, the cod line was tied up and thrown over the side. We were fishing again within fifteen minutes.

I noticed the old trimmer's hands were very cold and he had a job to untie the quarter rope. 'I shall have to watch him and see he doesn't drop it. It will lose us a lot of time if he does,' I thought. During our gutting I asked the old trimmer, who was my father in law, how many cod he had gutted in sixty years. He said he had gutted thousands of them. When I asked him

165.

how many fins a cod had, he said he'd be blowed if he knew, he'd never counted them.

It was not long after that the wind started to blow. The chief engineer complained that he could not reach any more coal in the stokehold. He had opened the wing doors to keep the fires burning, but he was afraid the coal would not last long enough and he wanted the coal trimming in the main bunkers. I asked the trimmer why the coal had not been trimmed. He told me he was not feeling too good.

As it was my watch off, I stripped off down to my waist and had two hours' hard work, getting the coal forward from the back of the bunkers, so that the engineers could reach the coal from the stokehold to keep the fires and steam at the right temperature. This gave the old trimmer plenty of time to rest and keep warm. Coming into dock the skipper told me to sack the old men so they could sign on the dole for the winter months. It was too dangerous for them working in the cold.

Finding good fishermen for North Sea vessels was a problem. Speaking to our ship's 'husband', Fred Standing, he said we had to anchor at the Burcombe Light Vessel and wait for trimmers and deck hands to be found. They would be brought to the ship by the tug *Brenda Fisher*, which had taken the old *Condor's* place.

Incidentally, the last time I saw the *Condor*, she was on the Mersey opposite the Liver buildings, with a square funnel–the only vessel I remember having ever seen with a square smoke stack–still being used as a tug.

Several vessels were now at anchor from various firms, all waiting for crews. The reason why we had to wait outside the docks, was because the firm then received a government grant of so much money per day while the ship was at sea. In dock, the firm received nothing. After being in the river for two days, we decided to go short-handed after asking the crew and telling them that they could share the missing crew's money between them. All agreed to catch a trip to bring home. The work was very hard, short-handed. We were glad when it was over and we were back in dock again.

Joe Grant, who had been third hand of the *S.T.Magnolia* when it sank, came as third hand with me on the *Rose.* We were brought up in the same street in Grimsby. One day I asked him what they were doing at the time I was in the wheelhouse steering, whilst towing the *Magnolia,* as I could not see anyone on their vessel. He told me they had been bailing out with buckets, trying to keep the water down, and when she sank the crew jumped overboard. Young Willis had gone down the forecastle and got trapped in there because the ship sank so quickly. The skipper was in his berth, speaking to the *Rose of England's* skipper at the time, and was also trapped in his cabin. Both were drowned.

We were fishing near the Silver Pits, on the south side, at twenty fathoms (a bit of rough ground) and we caught a few nice turbots amongst the plaice; dropping now and again in the deep water, at thirty-two fathoms we caught some soles. 'This is going to be a nice trip', I said to Joe, 'nice plaice, turbot, soles, couldn't do any better, and no split net for a change. We had found a tow with no fastenings, and there were fish to be caught. We started to tow towards the river, so that when we finished fishing, there would not be many miles to steam home.

As it was beginning to get dusk, Alf told me he wanted to tow between two wrecks, something we had done many times, sometimes catching a large bag of cod by doing this. Alf believed that the best time to go through them was now, when it was just beginning to get dark.

I could feel the doors on the trawl touching the wrecks, a small tug here, another little tug there, until we were clear. Hauling our gear up, the two doors first, we heard a swishing sound as the cod ends came out of the sea in a great big ball, full of large cod trying to get away from the net. It was too much weight to heave aboard, we had to halve the catch and make two bags of it.

We had the fish on deck in very quick time. Gutting it whilst the skipper steered for the River Humber, were Joe Grant, third hand; Harry Stratton, trimmer; young Yarbrough, deck hand; myself; and one more deck hand whose name I cannot now remember. The fish were washed and Harry went down the fishroom hatch to chop ice, ready for stowing the two hundred boxes of cod we now had on deck. I cannot ever recall a trip being caught in only ten days' fishing like this one. Most of the crew said they were going to buy new clothes with the poundage they would receive.

We came into the lock pits, the first vessel to enter the dock,

I felt proud of the tally I gave for our ship that day. Going home, I told my wife if the fish brought £3 a box we could not make less than £1,100. I would buy a new coat for her, and a suit for my boy.

Next morning all the crew turned up for the landing; roughly three hundred and twenty boxes from our ship. Sam Bee, fish salesman, with two more young salesmen from Franklin's firm, sold the fish.

Going down the dock at dinner time for my settling I met some of the crew. What they told me I cannot write down here, it is unprintable. We only made £850, so that we could claim the government grant.

With the *Magnolia* episode, I had to pay my share of expenses; towing time, and time at sea, so we did not receive one penny.

There was a row over the price the fish made, but I believe, for some unknown reason, we also paid for another ship's expenses. The money I received out of the trip was £5 per week, not a penny more, to keep the home going and buy my own sea gear and food. The skipper and mate had to pay for our own food on board; it was stopped out of the settling.

Many years later I received £13 back tax, for paying tax twice on my food. I often wonder how much back tax I was really owed by the tax people.

Some of the crew started owing money to the firm; they were subbing each trip and not making enough to pay it back, nor earning enough to live on. I was beginning to owe rent, we needed clothes to wear and I needed a new oil frock and boots. The oil frock I had was linseed oiled that many times, I saw no cotton to oil any more. My boots had had holes in them for a long time, and I could not go to sea without good sea gear.

The skipper had been on the docks for his bonus, which was received from Mr Franklin himself. The crew received nothing. We believed we would receive loss of earning money, or even loss of time money, but we were given nothing at all.

One of the firm's cooks, a nice chap, told me he had to leave the firm, because he owed £1,000. Today that figure would have been a lot higher.

Going home a bit dejected, I met another skipper who was very near to tears. (The last time I had seen him was in the Sparrow's Nest, 1939-40.) When I asked him what was wrong he told me that he had just been for his bonus, from his firm. Earlier he had left his wife in Riby Square, telling her that he would take her shopping when he received his bonus–but the gaffer told him there was none for him.

He got a job ashore and did not go to sea again.

Curley Cooper was out of a ship at the time and he asked me if we could find a job ashore until things sorted themselves out a bit. We hitched a ride to Scunthorpe. It was freezing very hard, and we found a temporary digging job in the steel works for Clugstons. Ted Cooper and I worked several weeks for Clugstons until the job was finished then we hitched a ride back to Grimsby.

We used to spend a bit of time cockling at Tetney, on the foreshore, until we decided to start fishing again. I noticed Deaf Tommy and his friends were together as usual, cockles being his lifelong friends.

Curly Kinch, the cook, who won a Purple Heart from America for saving an American airman, was ashore as well. They told me Curly Kinch had seen this airman in the cold sea off Iceland. Not hesitating, he dived from his ship and saved the man, whose parents later wanted Curly to visit America to be presented with the Purple Heart in the traditional manner. But Curly was no hero, he told the neighbours. It was a job, he did it and did not need to make a fuss about it.

Curly was a very good cook: he always went to sea in deep-water fishing ships. He seemed to have a fight every time he came into dock because he would get upset over something silly whilst drinking; he liked his beer. Curly married his girl friend late in life and quietened down a lot as he got older. When he died he was still a hero to all Grimsby fishermen, most of them knew him.

G. & F. Sleight's and Apples In My Sea Bag

When I left the old *Rose of England* I signed on one of the Sleights' North Sea trawlers. At one time, I remember, the firm had sixty-two vessels to manage. Sixty had names beginning with 'R' and ending with 'O'. Two others, I believe, began with 'S', the *S. T. Samuri* being one. It rammed a submarine during the war, I heard, outside the River Humber.

Fred Hodson had survived the war. How, I cannot say; the Lord must have kept an eye on him because he blew up more mines than anyone else. He just went hunting for them anywhere, on the shoals, out of the shipping lanes: wherever he looked he would find them. The ship's funnel was full of chevrons. He deserved a medal as big as a frying pan–but the Navy kicked him out and told him to go fishing again. Like Frank, his brother, he could not stand the discipline, the 'Yes, sir', 'No, sir'. The top brass clamped on them and sent them to fish again.

Fred Hodson and I got on well together. As skipper and mate we worked hard for a living with the firm expecting us to land once a week. Just enough food and stores were put on board for about seven days, so the cook always let the skipper know when we had to go home. Sometimes a vessel returning home earlier than planned, would give us a few rations if he had broken down or perhaps had a good catch. We would have an extra day's fishing then.

I saw the same kind of fishing as other firms did; the same mines, mine cradles (the support in which the mine was carried and which, after it had been laid, acted as an anchor for the mine), aircraft fuselages; the net being fished round the Yorkshire Hole, the Red House, or anywhere near wrecks–the closer the better. If the trawl became too torn to repair quickly, rather than lose too much time mending it we would change over from port side gear to starboard side gear: changing after each haul was common. We kept our otter doors outside by the gallows, all ready for a change over, and change over we did.

The firm did not mind the net being torn, as long as we didn't lose the gear altogether. In dock the net was repaired for us by net menders ready for sea again, but during the fishing we had to mend it ourselves. Tarry twine was still used then, tarry net for a large tear too.

We became very tired after a few days of this. Very little sleep was had by any of the crew. Winter time was the worst, with the cold freezing weather. We had very little sea gear because we couldn't afford it, we were only earning just enough money to live on. My wife and son and the crew's wives and families, were worse off than we were. Our sea woollens were mended at home after each trip, our oil frocks taken home to oil with burnt linseed oil, hanging in the back yard to dry. We didn't have many hours in dock before we were at sea again.

The crews were a mixed bunch of men from all different parts of the country. Miners tried to have a go; there were several Yanks who stayed for a while in this country before going back to America. There were some soldiers who made good fishermen when they had finished in the army. Sailors from all over the globe came to learn, then moved away to various other ports to fish. I only met one Jew who was daft enough to fish out of Grimsby.

Fishing for Sleights was a gamble for all of us. If we worked hard we got a living–but that was all. We had to keep fishing; sometimes we caught very little, at another time the bag would come floating to the surface full of fish–we would still be gutting whilst being moored in the dock with maybe several more ships in dock doing the same.

There have been times when we have come into the dock and I have moored the ship and gone home. I have returned for landing at 4.00 a.m. the next morning only to find the crew still asleep on the lockers in the fo'c'sle.. They had washed and cleaned up to go home after we came in dock but were so tired they had fallen asleep in the warm forecastle, not knowing that they were there.

Some of the crew were lucky to earn enough money for their 'baccy' as they called it. Sometimes I would catch a trimmer or deck hand in the galley mixing dry tea with his cigarette baccy to make it last longer.

The toilets in the old ship were still the same, we either had to sit on the ship's rail or the deck boads, and we had to be watched all the time while at sea. If anyone fell asleep while on the rail, and the ship rolled heavily, he might go over the side. I had small lines attached to the gallas for them to fasten themselves to. We had to keep our eyes on the older men all the time!

Crews became very scarce. We anchored longer than usual in the river for a crew to come out by tug. I remember waiting one night; when I was on watch the anchor cable snapped, the running tide was very fast that night. That was the only time I ever heard of a cable snapping.

CHRISTMAS TIME–AGAIN GOING TO SEA

Fred Hodson and I had several ship changes during the time we fished together. Hoddy asked me if I would go to sea for

Christmas with him in the *S.T. Reperio*. We had earned very little during the year, and Fred was not given any bonus money. My wife and I agreed to have a late Christmas after the trip.

We decided to pick a suitable crew to sail with us but everyone we spoke to wanted Christmas at home. So we had to take anyone willing to have Christmas at sea–the last scrapings from the barrel. None of them was known to us.

Just two days before Christmas we sailed from the North Wall, due to fish forty to sixty miles east from the River Humber. It was a nice morning. There was a bit of mist around, but the sea was very calm. Setting the log at Spurn Light Vessel, we set course for the fishing ground. I was on the bridge, still in my shore clothes, while dinner was being served up. The skipper, third hand, decky, first engineer and trimmer had dinner first sitting.

At 12.30 p.m. I was relieved by the third hand and decky coming on the bridge whilst the skipper went below to change into his working gear. I gave the third hand the course to steer and told him to call the skipper when fifty miles was clocked on the log. The weather, being clear with blue skies, we could see all round the horizon. There was only one vessel to be seen, approximately eight miles away on the starboard bow.

Going below, reading a paper, which I had taken from my sea bag, in my bunk, I also noticed that my wife had packed a small bag of apples with my sea clothes.

She had told me many times that apples would <u>not</u> be put in my sea bag again because, during my fishing time at sea, whenever we broke down, made a broken trip or something happened at sea, I always found apples were in my bag. So we made a pact, not to take apples to sea again. Many fishermen were superstitious about something or other, I guess this was mine.

However I put the bag of apples in my locker with my razor, soap, towel and other things.

Then I heard our ship's siren give one short blast, meaning

that we were to alter course to starboard. I thought to myself: 'Why?' Only one vessel had been on the horizon, miles away to starboard of us, when I left the bridge.

Bang!

I was knocked off the locker seat. Scrambling to the deck I looked forward, to see a large cargo ship passing our bow, steaming north-west.

The cargo boat continued steaming on its course. I looked at our bow–which was now facing aft. Opening the fore hold hatch I had a look down but could see no water coming into the ship, so I went down the chain locker to look further into the bow itself. There was just a small trickle coming through the bend. Coming back on deck I found the two mast stays lying there.

I had a word with the skipper, wanting to try to catch a trip but the crew wanted to return home. How or why we hit that ship I will never know. Didn't the third hand want Christmas at sea? Or was it my apples again?

CHAPTER 13

REMINISCENCES AGAIN

DURING MY EARLY DAYS FISHING IN THE OLD STEAM TRAWLERS I used to hear all kinds of stories about the past.

Dod Osborne stole the *Girl Pat,* a seine netter, from Grimsby. I must have been about ready to go to sea then. I can remember the song 'Red Sails in the Sunset' coming out about the same time and we bought a record of it.

I lived in Hainton Avenue for a while, two doors away from Dod's family. Later he was jailed for gun running and several more things. He finished up in Dakar on the coast of Africa. He certainly seemed to have a devil may care attitude !

Another skipper with whom I sailed in the old *S.T.Emerald* or *S.T.Diamond*, out of the T.C. & F. Moss firm, was called Jockey Grimmer. He told me about a skipper who, coming from the Faroes, put into Aberdeen on his way home. Having a few pints down him, he sold all the fish and the smack as well; it belonged to a Grimsby owner.

Young Arthur Bland took a vessel out of Grimsby Docks on his own, the seiner, *Ann,* to show the firm that the ship required only one man to work it. He made his point, because he knew his job and worked hard. He tried again but was caught and reprimanded

Talking to Arthur on the West Wall, I told him his father and I had been school pals. His father had a skipper's certificate, an engineer's ticket, and also a cook's certificate. Young Arthur had just landed a freelance photographer then working on a job for Calendar, the Yorkshire T.V. News. He had had several days out with Arthur and his wife Sandra, taking pictures.

Arthur told me the people who say the river is polluted must be mad. There were all the fish you can mention, that normally live around our coast, in the river, even herrings had been caught in his net. He also told me that something kept snagging his net and he would like to know what it was. I believe they were the only two married people to live and fish together on the east coast.

Whilst writing these stories, I regret to say that Arthur and his wife Sandra have been lost off the small fishing trawler *Emma*, a 33ft. wooden-built vessel bought by them to fish the River Humber. The two of them were running the vessel on their own, landing the catch several times a week, weather permitting.

Just after the war I was fishing in the White Sea. Icing the ship at Tromsö, the skipper signed three Norwegians for gutting the fish. Seeing them come on board I asked where their fishing clothes were as they carried very small bags with them. They replied that their oil frocks were in these small parcels. They seemed to be very quiet, and looked a bit crafty, so our crew watched them.

When we arrived on the fishing grounds and had our first haul, the three of them came on deck dressed in German diving suits instead of oil frocks. They said it was their working clothes. We had not expected this, but they said the Germans had left the suits so they were going to use them. While we were washing the fish and dropping it down the hatch, I saw one of the Norwegians fall over frothing at the mouth. Another complained of pains in his chest. The other one cut through his diving suit and had difficulties breathing. They all finished up wearing our crew's old gear.

At the last haul, the Norwegians requested that they each should take twenty red fish, soldiers as we called them (red bream now), back home with them. They picked sixty of the largest reds they could find and tied a line through each gill of ten, making six heaps near the forward starboard gallows. These froze in one solid lump on the way back to Tromsö. The weather was beginning to get worse with storms and gale force winds which blew the fiord entrance light away. We had to dodge outside Tromsö Fiord until the skipper decided to head for home on the outside coast of Norway. I opened our fishing hatch and dropped the sixty reds onto the stage in the fishroom, after the weather abated.

Arriving in Grimsby, I was surprised to find the police waiting for us. They took the three Norwegians to Sunderland straight away and sent them home by boat, without a chance to stay in Britain. We landed the sixty reds which were sold. No reds had been landed in Grimsby before, for sale by auction.

They have been landed and sold as bream ever since, a nice tasty fish full of oil. The Norwegians knew this.

I can recall the names of most steam trawlers that sailed out of Grimsby but I was too young to remember the smacks sailing from there.

Remembering some of the old cod men who lived near me, one, a Mr Hammer, showed me how to take a hook out of your arm–or any part of the body. The hooks flying around as the winch brought the lines and fish in were dangerous. When he went fishing at Greenland, he was away for many weeks.

I saw a few of Grimsby's smacks in the Faroe Islands, whilst sheltering from bad weather. *Robert the Devil* was on one ship's stern, cut into the wood, with 'Grimsby' under the name. The vessel was rotted when I saw it, around sixty years ago.

Some of the crews I sailed with are still with us. Skipper Harold Brennan, past his eighties, still loves a pint of beer in his local, the Clee Park Hotel. A grand old Faroe Bank fisherman.

I know that there are some of the old Danish, Swedes, Scotch, Dutch, and Belgian fishermen still living in Grimsby or Cleethorpes. These and the countless Grimsby fishermen put the 'Great' into it.

There were one hundred and ten pubs and clubs, two missions, and a port missionary.

Despite such a small wage, we had a smile, a laugh, and sometimes a tear.

We carried on until the steam trawler was a legend, like the men.

* * * * *

Thinking back, we sometimes had something to smile about; such as the skipper who played the violin whilst leaving port. he would play his violin singing, to the tune of a well-known song:

> *Last night you called me a so and so,*
> *Tonight you belong to me.*

He would also play, to a well known tune: *Just an old-fashioned trawler, with an old-fashioned crew, and the skipper says 'Welcome' to you,* and so on. I have forgotten all the words now, but he gave the lads some stick at sea.

There was old Bing Beales, the variety comic. Who could think Bing went to sea as a fisherman? He sailed with me in the Steam Trawler *Strephon* before the war. It belonged to W.W. Butts. Later it went into Taylor's firm where Mr Fisher, a very tall man, was the ship's runner. He started the idea of a taxi to pick the crew up from home.

Bing was to be picked up at 2.00 a.m. He lived in the old skippers' homes in Orwell Street, large houses for large families. Unknown to Bing, his wife would sub-let the attics upstairs while he was at sea.

Mr Fisher had a few drinks while travelling around in the taxi, going back and forth to different vessels wanting to leave for the fishing grounds, and each skipper gave him a tot before leaving his home for the docks. Calling at Bing's home, and knocking very hard at the door, he found it was opened by a Sikh in his Indian religious clothing, white from head to toe.

Mr Fisher saw this 'ghost' and fled, the taxi going at great speed down the docks. He never went for Bing again. We had to wait in the river for a crew to be brought out by the *Brenda Fisher*, the section tug.

I spoke to Bing in dock the next trip, and he told me the Indian Sikh was living in his attic but he had not not known that his wife had sub-let it. Bing saw the Sikh taking a young goat upstairs and asked him what he intended to do with it. The Sikh told him it was for a sacrifice. Bing replied in fisherman's language that he was not to kill it upstairs.

About the same time, I was in Fish Dock Road when I saw a taxi in the middle of the road, stopped. John Marsdon, later Sir John, was talking to a well-known skipper, a top earner, who was sitting on the taxi step and crying like a child, saying he did not want to join his ship which was at anchor in the river waiting for him. He wanted more time at home. His wife and daughter were trying to persuade him to go to sea.

Many fishermen felt like him, but had to go. It was the only job they knew.

The old *Cineraria* was a very old seine netter out of Franklins' firm, made of iron, including the decks too. I sailed as mate in this vessel. The skipper came from Lowestoft.

Using only nine ropes we had eight short hauls per day. We fished mostly on the hills, about forty to fifty miles east of Flamborough Head. Catching a few codling, I told the skipper I had been overhauling the spare net in the hold and I could see a very old haddock net. I had never seen one used before and would like to use it and catch some cod and codlings. His remark about this surprised me; he told me it would not catch a lot of fish and was not worth the trouble to fix it up. The weather was fine and warm, we were only catching a basket of plaice a haul, and the odd codling. He saw I was a bit disappointed and told me if I would like to fix the haddock net up, we could try it.

It was much bigger than I had thought, the meshes only being about one inch square. I remember putting thirty to forty headline cans on the net, six feet apart. Anyway we shot the net, heaving it back again. I was hoping we had caught a lot of fish. Seeing the bag come up, it was a sight to see. Letting the cod line drift, tiny fish teemed on to the deck, filling all the fish pounds up to the rail.

I could only stand and stare, I could not believe it.

The skipper and crew were laughing their heads off. 'I told you', the skipper said. 'Take it off and put the other net back on again.'

The fish we had caught were all baby fish, most of the plaice, dabs and bully heads were no more than two or three inches long, two whitings were about five inches long. We put the donkey hose among the fish and washed them all back into the sea again. We dried the haddock net and put it down the hold again.

I had learnt a lesson.

THE HEADLESS COD

Sailing in several ships of Sleights with Fred Hodson, we still could not make a lot of money. We worked hard; the crews were the older men now, the younger chaps wanting to go into the big ships. Some of the deep water vessels made a nice trip but it wasn't the amount of fish brought in that made the money. Small amounts brought in quickly when you had no competition made the money. Foreign ships bringing fish into Grimsby anchored off the Humber until very few of our ships were due in. They always seemed to get a good market.

Anyway the fishermen I knew told me if they did not make a good trip there was always the liver money to look forward to, whereas in the North Sea we did not have many livers to save. Then, they said, the bonded stores on the big ships were a big help too.

I left Fred Hodson and signed on the Steam Trawler *Visenda,* one of the Lettons' firm's ships   I did not know any of the crew and I didn't like going to Iceland either. My wife didn't like me going, but she needed clothes and my lad required things I could not buy him. My sea gear wasn't up to standard. Not being able to buy any more, I went, as we called it, schooner rigged.

Sailing from Grimsby Docks, the watch set, we rigged the life lines fore and aft, and went on the bridge for our bonded stores. Approximately eighty hours later we were fishing in Icelandic waters. A few small Icelandic liners were in our vicinity, and when we hauled on the otter doors we could see codlings, haddocks, all kinds of fish hanging on the lines around the doors, all hooked fish. The skipper screamed to us to chop the lines away.

As we were to head all our fish this trip, on orders from the office, the ship's husband had had a couple of dozen large heavy knives sent on board with which to chop the cods' heads off. These we used to chop the fish and lines off the doors. The knives were useless to chop the head from a cod. Laying the cod on the warp with its belly up, pressing the head back smartly, it came off in seconds, a lot quicker than hacking it off with a knife.

We caught a lot of cod and codling. The small fish we booted through the scuppers. I thought, if I could only have caught some of these in the old haddock net.

Our wrists were beginning to show the strain and became twice their normal size. We were working eighteen hours on deck, with six hours rest below. This was new to me. I had been used to going to bed only on the way home, staying on deck almost all the time until full up. I was forgetting this ship held three times more fish than the vessels in which I had been to the White Sea.

The mate told the skipper that we were about full up with headless cod, three thousand kits he said he would tally. The trip was caught in about eighteen days' fishing. Steaming home, I thought I was in the Navy again, polish this, polish that, grease the portholes after you have polished them. The skipper's stairway really glistened with the cod liver oil that was used to polish it. Even the two large ventilators were polished, decks scrubbed with caustic powder, baskets and net cleaned and stowed away like a sailor's hammock.

I noticed the vessel took a lot of water amidships. She rolled very badly and I did not like the way she behaved. Some of the crew said she was a dirty b . . . . . . and had always been like it.

Going through the Pentland Firth, about abreast of Dunnet Head, I sat on the skylight, for'ard, just under the whaleback. I could hear the crew playing cards, laughing and carrying on as they do, when all at once the ship started to run herself under. I shouted to them to come up on deck; the water was up to the top of the winch.

The skipper stopped the engines and the vessel, now motionless, started to shudder and came up again. The fishrooms were full up, there was no air for any buoyancy. The bunkers were getting low now, the coal having been used up, so there must be air down there, I was thinking to myself. I heard the telegraph, slow speed ahead.

In about ten minutes, she started to run under again. The engines stopped once more. Coming up, we waited until the decks cleared of water, then rang slow speed ahead again.

This time all was O.K. We had got caught in the Bores, seven tides that meet in the Pentland Firth. None of the crew left their game of cards. They just would not believe what I was telling them.

When we rounded Duncansby Head, full steam was given. We landed 3,300 kits of headless cod, most of it going to the fishmeal factory. As the crew said, the liver oil money came in handy.

I did not go in that ship any more.

I signed on the *S.T. Strephon*, one of the Taylors' North Sea vessels. It used to be in W.W. Butts' firm as one of their Faroe ships.

182.

Near Christmas again, we fished in the Great Silver Pits, where some years previously we had caught many baskets of soles per haul. This time we fished in thirty-two fathoms. Our old depth finder kept going on the blink, the skipper said the batteries were down. Anyway, the old lead line came in handy and we kept in the thirties, catching up to eight baskets of good big plaice each haul, which was very good then. They were very thick, these plaice, the spots on them looked as if someone had just painted them red.

The first trip on them we made £1,100 which was very good for those days. Several times we went to the same spot, dropping a dan buoy. We made £1,500 and a £1,200 just before Christmas. It was the best Christmas we had for years. Not one mine, bomb, piece of wreckage or anything to hinder the fishing.

Some queer things were picked up and seen after gales of wind. Large Russian ships would pass us loaded with timber. Sometimes, after a gale, they would be listing badly, caused by the waves wetting the timber on the weather side, and they looked very funny steaming on one side.

'Dodging' our ship in the Silver Pits during bad weather I saw a signpost pass by. It must have blown out of some farmer's field and into the water. It read: 'Please close the gate'.

After Christmas we had some awful weather. We had to lay-to in deep water for many days. Some of the cargo boats lost cargo off their decks.

I remember, whilst hauling, we once picked a Christmas tree up in the net and, during some fine weather, I climbed to the trock of the mainmast, pulled it up and made it fast, sticking it up at the mast top. When we came into the dock, Harold Moss asked me who put the Christmas tree on top of the mast. I told him that I did. He walked off, saying I must be mad. It was there for several trips until someone cut it down and took it home for the kids at Christmas.

My old father-in-law brought a bag of oranges home for the

kids after picking up several cases floating nearby. Ships sometimes picked up cases full of oranges and brought them into port. Many were sold for a few pence on Freeman Street market.

Cases of pottery were sometimes picked up by inshore fishing vessels. One of my neighbours, fishing on the Dogger edge, caught a large crate in the net. Breaking the wooden lats, they found dozens of teapots, coffee jugs, of all different designs. He told me only one or two were broken, as they were packed in straw. We had teapots, coffee jugs, sugar bowls and other items to give to the neighbours in our street.

I remember catching soles in the great Silver Pits, ten to fifteen baskets a haul, all dead. The big frost had killed them and their eyes were white. Ships came into the dock frozen up, breaking up the frozen water as they came into the dock. Ice floes ten miles long were reported off Sheringham.

Several trawlers had to go home, damaged by the heavy seas. One trawler, returning from Iceland, found a derelict coal cargo vessel, the crew having been taken off by lifeboat. The mate of the trawler made a very daring jump and got on to the abandoned vessel's bow. Somehow they managed to make a tow, towing the ship to Hull. What a prize!

I remember a man being hurt after being caught between the life boat and the coal ship, and being taken to hospital.

We did not find much fish in the new Year. The skipper got fed up and it took a long time to wake him up at hauling time. The third hand would take six to eight hours to get him out. He got worse, trip after trip.

After I left the *Strephon*, Alf asked me to go back in the *Rose of England* again. Fred Standing was the ship's runner for Harry Franklin and he signed me on the log book. During the time *Rose* had a refit–the tubes were always being repaired, she was getting old now–Fred Standing would ask me to go in one of their seiners. I went in several of these, doing a trip here, a trip there.

One trip, one of the seiners fishing nearby had lost her propellor. We had to tow the vessel home. The same year I was in that vessel which I had towed home, when the other one lost **her** propellor. So we had to tow home the vessel which had towed ours only a few months before.

Mr Knudd had come to Grimsby from Lowestoft, he was the skipper of the old *Viscaria*, an iron seiner. I sailed in this vessel with Knuddy when he won three and a half thousand pounds on the football coupons. He bought me a bottle of rum out of his winnings.

Knuddy had a lad who went to sea but was out of a ship when his dad won the money. I was with Knuddy at twelve o'clock, dinner time, when he gave his lad fifty pounds for himself. At five p.m. the lad asked his dad for more money, he had spent the lot. Beer was sixpence a pint, whisky eight pence a glass.

Going to sea in the *M.V. Viscaria*, Knuddy had begun fishing forty miles due east of Flamborough lighthouse when the wind started to blow hard from the north-west. He hauled the anchor up and fouled it, before dropping it again. He thought that if he did this, the anchor would drag and not pull the bows off, nor break the anchor cable.

Only a compass and leadline, ship's log line and clock were available for navigation; the weed and any flotsam caught in the net, together with the type of sea-bed revealed by the base of the lead, told him where he was when fishing.

The wind blew stronger, all the deck boards were wedged in place, baskets and nets stowed and made fast. As the weather became gale force, the crew became worried and closed the hatch on the cabin hoodway.

For three days and nights, during this north-westerly gale, no one dared come on deck. The wind dropped all at once on a Sunday morning. Opening the hatch door and looking on deck we saw that it had been swept clean: no net, no deck boards, no baskets. To the east the skipper could see the Ville

Lightship. The *Viscaria* had dragged its anchor all the way across the North Sea.

After the gale I talked to a seiner cook who had had to anchor for seven days in the North Sea. On the Sunday morning after the gales, he wanted to use the toilet. Going on deck, it surprised him to see the water was as flat as a pancake, and no wind. He reported this to the skipper, who told him to make a pot of tea and he would take a look-see.

Shooting the net before daylight, they started to heave it back again. All was going well until the last ropes were coming in, at breaking point. The skipper slowed the winch down and began to heave very slowly, looking over the side waiting for the net to show. He told the crew he suspected they had picked up a mine, or mine cradle, and he was being careful.

A little later, looking again into the water, he saw several plaice swimming to the top. 'It could be fish' he said with a grin. When the net did eventually come to the surface, it was a very large bag of plaice, all good fish. The tackle and jilson had to be used to bring the it inboard. Just as it came aboard the bag burst, sending the plaice all round the ship and causing some of the weaker planks to burst with the weight of fish.

Pound boards from the fish room were quickly nailed to stop the flow of fish going back into the sea. Coming home after the one haul the ship made over £1,100–which was a lot of money in those days.

After the gales more fish seemed to be caught. One seiner caught a large bag of cod. Trying to bring a good big bag up in one heave, the mast came down breaking at the foot. The skipper decided to tow the net and cod alongside the ship until they were safely in the river, where the fish was brought aboard bit by bit, gutted and put below, on ice.

Many times during my fishing days we caught large bags of roker skate and dog fish, which were very hard to split to make into two bags. The third hand would untie the knot in the cod line to let the fish out on deck. Nothing would happen, the fish being rough and dry, stayed put. We had to cut the cod ends and pull the fish out one by one until we could shake them out.

We did not gut the dogs, only the large skate; the small ones did not make a lot of money, gutted or not. I remember a fish buyer buying approximately thirteen stones of monk's tails we had caught. He gave thirty shillings for them on the dock market, I saw them in his shop at 2s 10d per pound.

I did not remain seine netting for long. I had a try to earn some money in Ron Bannister's firm. I saw young Fred Ireland was skipper in the firm, and went mate with him. I believe the vessel was *War Duke,* built in 1917 and now in this firm, after being with a number of other firms. Fred's brother was a skipper for the same company too.

We fished quite a lot on the limit line, sometimes sneaking inside to see if anything was worth catching. I can remember some of the crew on board: Mr Pike was the cook I mentioned in Chapter 15, the huge young Helston was deck hand with his pal, a very small man, whom Helston carried about on his shoulders, whilst his pal held a basket full of coal for the fo'castle, climbing over the deck boards at the same time.

We caught many lobsters inside the limit at one time–one hundred and fifty odd we caught on one haul with lobsters inside and outside the net. Mr Pike was called out and promised a bag full of lobsters if he cooked them for us to take home. We soon became fed up with eating lobster on board, as did the people in my street. Asking my neighbours if they wanted any lobsters, I could not give them away. Some I put into the refuse bin.

The prawns that Mr Pike cooked for us we took home in pillowslips-full. The kids loved to take these to school, eating them like sweets. Queens and whelks were put into the jars we took to sea with us ready for them. Also the jars were used for beef dripping which the cooks saved and which we took home to use on our bread.

Large loaves would be cooked by Mr Pike, who lived in

Tunnard Street, Grimsby, for all the crew to take one apiece. We looked after Mr Pike, cleaning his fish during the night and cleaning his galley fire for him, and in return he did a lot for us. I enjoyed my time with Fred, he was well-liked by his crew.

'Old' Harold Moss, still ship's husband for the T.C. & F. Moss Company, wanted me to sail in his firm again. He told me that young Tom Moss wanted to speak to me. Going into the office, I sat on leather seats polished so that you could see yourself in them. Young Tom asked me what I wanted. I said that his Uncle Harold had sent me to see him, saying he wanted to speak to me. He looked at me for a second, went to the safe and gave me a five pound note. ''Op it', he said. Five pounds was a lot of money then.

I sailed in Moss's firm until I finished going to sea because my wife became ill and needed someone to take care of my boy.

*   *   *   *   *   *

AT THE END OF THE DAYS

During the fifties many fishermen left the fishing industry and found jobs ashore. Scunthorpe was a town where a number of jobs became available. My boy now required work of some sort and his mother was begging me not to take him to sea. We both decided to look for work outside Grimsby.

Hitch-hiking to Scunthorpe we met many Grimsby ex-fishermen who put us on the right track. We saw Grimsby men who had become foremen of building site work, men who, like me, knew only about the sea, gutting fish and mending nets. It surprised me that these men could become charge hands at scaffolding, first class men who now earned good money in regular work. There were not only Grimsby men. I spoke to a Scottish herring fisherman I had met on a boat landing herrings in the basin. He told me he came from Fraserburgh and he was a joiner at Scunthorpe. He went to sea again for the herring season and back to Scunthorpe after the herrings had gone.

It seemed to me that the Irishmen, who were often the works foremen and managers, liked the fishermen and gave them work because they worked hard and were always on time for work, which was appreciated.

When one job finished, another firm would take us on. This way we always had a wage coming in at the end of the week. We could buy food, clothes, pay the rent and buy coal for our fire. I took up fishing in a different way–on my days off from work I went with my rod and line to the West Pier, Royal Dock Basin, having paid for my fishing licence from the dock offices, and spent many a happy hour there fishing.

Whilst I was working at Scunthorpe, I sometimes went to the works canteen for my meals. For one shilling we could have a good dinner.

A young chap came and sat alongside me. We began talking to each other. He told me he came from the Midlands and wanted a job. I advised him not to go to the firm he was intending to and told him (in fishermen's language) what that firm was like. Instead, I said that he should see our foreman, who would set him on.

He told me he only required a job for six weeks. He was a priest and wanted to know how the other side lived. I apologised to him for swearing but he said it was O.K., it would be his first lesson, that's what he had been sent here for.

Another story: I had to work at Immingham Docks for a company. We visited the Flying Angel mission for a cuppa during the morning breaks, the reverend making the tea or coffee for us. One morning, going into the mission for my coffee, the superintendent sat in his chair, very upset, nearly in tears. When I asked why he was so miserable, he replied that someone had broken all the knobs off the urn which was used to boil the water. He had the water boiling, but no way could he turn the taps on. He had tried using a pair of pliers but that did not work.

I told him to stay put, I would be gone about ten minutes and be back.

Going to our stores, I picked three small wheels and three small bolts I thought might do the trick. At the Mission I put the three wheels on the urn where the three small square rods were sticking out. They fitted like a glove. Putting the three bolts in the holes, they fitted too. I could not believe it, he couldn't either. 'Turn it on,' I said.

He gave me a coffee and would not take the twopence. He asked me where I had got them from. I told him I pinched them out of our stores. He looked at me, then up to the ceiling, replying: 'Nothing is ever stolen as long as it is given to a friend.'

Another time, whilst I was in the mission sitting near the telephone having my coffee, the telephone bell rang. The mission officer, answering the phone, asked who was speaking. A voice asked, very loud and clear: 'Are you Jesus?'

The mission officer was taken aback a bit and said: 'Well, not quite. Who do you want?'

'Jesus', was the reply.

A man sitting near me jumped up and going up to the mission officer said in broken English: 'Me Jesus. My friend on telephone, me waiting for him with message.' He was from one of the vessels in the Immingham Dock.

Which reminds me of our own mission and their officers. What would the fishermen have done without their help?

Ten thousand fishermen and just a handful of officers. Riby House was always open to all seafaring men. The work these officers did, and still do, should be recognised more widely. I'm sure the work they do, every day of the year, would qualify them for some kind of a medal.

Thousands of fishermen's wives have been comforted by these mission officers, and the fishermen themselves, when in trouble of some kind, look to the mission for help.

The port missionary has his sombre work to do too, as you can see by the names on mission walls. New names, same story, lost at sea. The missionary has to go to work again.

Like, Paddy, George Newse, Bill Redgrift, the Hodson brothers, Len Brown, Fred Howson, Tommy Cutler, Alf Walker, Snowy Wing.

They were all good fishermen; deep sea, North Sea, inshore, they all brought their fish into Grimsby Fish Docks.

I was younger yesterday than I am today. We live in the Fishermen's Home now, too old to work the ships any more.

I have only to look down our street to see the greatest sight in the world. To all fishermen, our own memorial to those who died.

The Grimsby Dock Tower